MEDIA LITERACY
THINKING CRITICALLY ABOUT
VISUAL CULTURE

Peyton Paxson

WALCH PUBLISHING

1   2   3   4   5   6   7   8   9   10

ISBN 0-8251-4991-6

Copyright © 2004
Walch Publishing
P.O. Box 658 • Portland, Maine 04104-0658
walch.com

Printed in the United States of America

Contents

A 1991 STUDY PUBLISHED in the *Journal of the American Medical Association* found that about 91 percent of six-year-olds surveyed recognized cigarette advertising icon Joe Camel—about the same number of six-year-olds that recognized the Mickey Mouse logo on the Disney Channel. The recognition rate of Joe Camel among three-year-olds was about 30 percent.[1]

It is a truism to state that there are economic and social consequences for people who can or cannot read written words. There are also significant consequences for people who can or cannot read symbolic imagery and behavior, just as there are important ramifications of people's ability or inability to recognize the various agendas that attend symbolic imagery and behavior.

This book, the sixth in a series on media literacy, focuses on visual culture. The effort here is to help students understand the complex social, economic, political, and personal foundations of visual culture. Each unit introduces students to the different contexts in which visual culture exists and functions. The activity sheets require students to recognize these contexts and demonstrate their understanding of the role that visual culture plays in each. The central principle of this book is that visual culture can be used to help students improve their critical-thinking skills.

---

[1] P. M. Fischer, M. P. Schwartz, J. W. Richards Jr., A. O. Goldstein, and T. H. Rojas, "Brand Logo Recognition by Children Aged 3 to 6 Years: Mickey Mouse and Old Joe the Camel." *Journal of the American Medical Association* 266, no. 22 (1991): 3145–3148.

MOST OF WHAT WE SEE every day we have seen before. We are often able to understand new things because they look similar to things we have seen before. There are many factors that contribute to the way we see things. The culture we grow up in is one of the most important factors. For example, when most Americans see a crawling bug, they may think "Oh, gross." In some other cultures, the bug may be seen as food. As our needs, attitudes, and interests vary, so do the ways that we perceive visual items.

Much of the information we need to survive and be happy is transmitted through the written word. You already know the ability to read and write is an important part of literacy. The fact that you can read these words demonstrates that you already possess this type of literacy. However, we also possess other types of literacy. For instance, in the years before the average resident of London, England, could read or write, she or he could still recognize the sign for British pubs (similar to restaurants or taverns), that used symbols, not words. Thus, an otherwise illiterate Londoner in the 1400s could find a meal at the Rose and Crown or at the Brown Dog, because of the symbols on their signs. Similarly today, the average citizen of the world does not need to be able to read English, nor any other language, to recognize McDonald's golden arches.

This book discusses a different type of literacy: visual literacy. Visual literacy includes not just our ability to understand the written word, but also symbols, the design and arrangement of objects, and people's appearances and behaviors. This book is designed to help you to develop your visual literacy—to better understand visual culture and how it affects your life.

There are probably several words in this book with which you are not familiar. You will find a glossary at the back of the book. Words that are defined in the glossary are highlighted in bold when introduced in the book.

The objectives of this unit are to help students

- appreciate the importance of visual culture in human society
- recognize that different people and different societies have different uses for visual culture
- understand the impact of technology on visual culture over time

DAVID CONSIDINE, coordinator of the media literacy project at Appalachian State University, states, "if we teach [students] to become critical viewers, we do more than give them the ability to analyze the construction of isolated images; we also give them the ability to think critically about the composition of the picture, enhancing their ability to read words and worlds."

This unit investigates the nature of human vision, and includes historical and multicultural approaches to help students examine how societies communicate visually.

In this Unit. . .

Blindness has students evaluate the relative advantages and disadvantages of blindness and deafness.

The Blind Person and the Airplane gives students the task of writing a description of a large jet airliner that would help a blind person understand what it looks like. Before writing, students must organize and evaluate important facts and consider the most appropriate method of conveying those facts to a person who is blind.

Technology and Literacy: The 1400s introduces students to Johannes Gutenberg's contributions to printing technology. Students are asked to analyze some of the social changes that resulted in Europe as the result of less expensive and more widely available printed materials.

Technology and Literacy: The 1800s has students assess the relationship between the Industrial Revolution and literacy.

Mechanical Reproduction and Visual Representation asks students to describe the benefits of technological devices that help people "see" phenomena we are otherwise unable to see.

The Multinational Logo involves students in the creation of a logo that would serve a common purpose in a variety of cultures and languages.

Design a Sign is suggested as a group project. Students are asked to create a universal sign to help foreign visitors locate an immigration document at the airport.

What Is Art? has students investigate the nature of art and to distinguish aesthetic imagery and documentary imagery.

"The Wall"—the Vietnam Veterans Memorial has students look at the controversy that accompanied Maya Lin's design of the Vietnam Veterans Memorial.

AS LONG AS HUMAN BEINGS have had eyes, we have had visual culture. Humans began to record and communicate information and ideas using symbols many thousands of years ago. Some of the evidence of early visual culture that has survived over the years includes etchings and drawings on stones and rocks. These petroglyphs (Greek for "stone carvings") are over thirty thousand years old. The printing press, which allowed writing to be reproduced quickly and relatively inexpensively, was probably invented within the last seven hundred years. Technology has significantly changed visual culture during the last two hundred years. Photography was invented in the early 1800s; motion photography (cinematography) was invented in the late 1800s. Television was popularized in the late 1940s. The Internet gained the ability to show graphics in the 1990s.

> **"As long as human beings have had eyes, we have had visual culture."**

Visual culture does not just "happen." People usually have reasons (an agenda) for creating visual culture. Likewise, people have reasons for viewing visual culture. These reasons may be ideological—they may involve politics or religion, for example. These reasons may be aesthetic—visual culture is often artistic. Visual culture is often created and consumed for commercial purposes. Visual culture also provides important information as well as relaxation and entertainment.

Blindness -

SOME PEOPLE ARE BLIND. They may be able to see some light or some shapes. However, they cannot see most of the things that sighted people can see. Some people are deaf. They may be able to hear some noises, and can often feel the vibrations that some sounds make. However, they cannot hear most of the things that hearing people can hear.

Record your answers below. Use another sheet of paper, if necessary.

1. Imagine that you suddenly become either blind or deaf. Which of the two do you think would cause you to make the most changes in your everyday life? Explain your answer.

   - What one activity in your life would be the most affected by being deaf? Explain why.

   - What one activity in your life would be the most affected by being blind? Explain why.

2. There are some people who argue that a deaf person should not be considered disabled. Instead, they say deafness is a culture of its own. Deaf people share a culture and a language (sign language) with other deaf people, just as speakers of English share a culture and a language with other English speakers.

   - Do you believe that the characterization of deafness as a culture can apply to a similar characterization of blindness? In other words, do you believe that blind people are disabled, or are they simply members of a different culture? Explain your answer.

3. Some sighted teenagers are quick to say they would have no problem dating a blind person. They are surprised to find out that some blind people do not want to date sighted people. Why do you think a blind person might not want to date a sighted person? List and describe three reasons.

The Blind Person and the Airplane -

THERE IS AN OLD TALE from India that you may have heard before. Six people, all born blind, had heard the sighted villagers speak often about elephants. However, none of the six really knew what an elephant was like. One day, a villager brought an elephant to the six blind people so that they could learn what an elephant was like.

> The first blind person reached out and touched the side of the huge animal. "An elephant is smooth and solid like a wall!" she declared. "It must be very powerful."

> The second blind person put his hand on the elephant's limber trunk. "An elephant is like a giant snake," he announced.

> The third blind person felt the elephant's pointed tusk. "This creature is as sharp and deadly as a spear."

> The fourth blind person touched one of the elephant's four legs. "What we have here," he said, "is an extremely large cow."

> The fifth blind person felt the elephant's giant ear. "I believe an elephant is like a huge fan or maybe a magic carpet that can fly over mountains and treetops," she said.

> The sixth blind person gave a tug on the elephant's fuzzy tail. "Why, this is nothing more than a piece of old rope. Dangerous, indeed," he scoffed.

This story is aimed primarily at sighted persons. The lesson here is that one has to put all the pieces of evidence together before she or he makes a decision about something.

A blind person can get a good sense of a smaller animal, such as a dog. The blind person can feel the dog's teeth, can rub their hands through the dog's fur, and can get a good sense of the overall size of the dog by placing their hands on the dog. Through the senses of smell and hearing, the blind person knows that many dogs do not smell too good, and that some dogs bark. However, for larger animals, the story of the elephant reminds us that the blind person's ability to understand the animal is more difficult.

Similarly, a blind person cannot develop a complete sense of a large object, such as a jet airliner, without some assistance. Your task is to write a description of a large jet airliner, such as a Boeing 747 or an Airbus A-340. The goal here is to create a description that, if read to a blind person, would enable him or her to understand what the plane looks like.

Before beginning your description, organize and evaluate your information.

(continued)

The Blind Person and the Airplane -------------------

Record your answers below. Use another sheet of paper, if necessary.

1. Identify information about a large jet airliner that *is not* necessary for this description. What information about a large jet airliner is factual but not important for your description? List three items, and explain why each is not important.

    •

    •

    •

2. Identify information about a large jet airliner that *is* necessary for this description. What basic facts about the plane do you think are important for your description? List five items, and explain why each is important.

    •

    •

    •

    •

    •

Once you have organized and evaluated your information about a large jet airliner, it is important to consider how you will share significant facts with a person who cannot see. For example, a Boeing 747 loaded with fuel, cargo, and passengers weighs more than 850,000 pounds. A blind person does not know what 850,000 pounds (425 tons) looks like or feels like. (And, unless you have been run over by a car, you probably do not have a sense of what a ton feels like, either.) However, a blind person has an understanding of weight in a smaller scale. She or he probably

(continued)

The Blind Person and the Airplane - - - - - - - - - - - - - - - - - -

knows what something that weighs one pound feels like, and a blind person may know that a gallon of water weighs around $8\frac{1}{2}$ pounds. Therefore, you could describe the Boeing 747 as equal in weight to 100,000 gallons of water.

For each of the five facts you have listed as important, consider how best to describe those facts in terms that can be understood by a person who cannot see what you are talking about, but who has the other basic senses (including hearing and touch) as well as some sense of weight and size.

3. Once you have organized and evaluated your information about a large jet airliner, and thought about how best to convey that information to a blind person, write a description of the plane that will help a blind person understand what it looks like.

Technology and Literacy: The 1400s -----------------

JOHANNES GUTENBERG, who lived in Germany from approximately 1400 to 1468, is commonly credited with being the first European to invent moveable type and develop the printing press sometime around 1450. (Many historians have argued that the printing press was invented perhaps six hundred years earlier in China.) Gutenberg's inventions allowed books and other material involving printed words to be mass-produced. Prior to this period, books had to be written by hand, a slow and an expensive process.

Record your answers below. Use another sheet of paper, if necessary.

1. Before Gutenberg's development of the printing press, relatively few people were able to read. Explain why you think this was so.

2. The first book Gutenberg is known to have printed was the Bible. Explain why you think he chose that book to be his first printed project.

3. Before Gutenberg's development of the printing press, most of the few people who were able to read were either rich people or religious leaders. Explain why you think this was so.

4. After Gutenberg's development of the printing press, more people who were not rich learned to read. How do you think the rich people felt about this? Explain your answer.

5. It has been said, "information is power." Explain what you think this means.

6. What effect do you think the invention of the printing press had on the distribution of power among different groups of people? In other words, do you think that power remained concentrated among a few important people, or do you think power began to spread among many people? Explain your answer.

Technology and Literacy: The 1800s - - - - - - - - - - - - - - - -

IN THE 1800s, the United States experienced the Industrial Revolution. This was a period known for the rapid invention and spread of new manufacturing technology. The Industrial Revolution caused an important shift in the American economy. Prior to this time, agriculture was the largest source of jobs for Americans. Within a few decades, manufacturing became Americans' largest source of employment.

Answer the following questions. Use another sheet of paper, if necessary.

In 1852, Massachusetts was the first state to adopt compulsory (required) education of children. By 1900, thirty-eight (of the then forty-five) states had compulsory education laws.

1. How did compulsory education laws benefit workers?

2. How did compulsory education laws benefit employers?

One of the activities that saw significant changes during the Industrial Revolution was printing. As the result of printing advances, it became easier and less expensive to make printed packages. This meant that companies that manufactured products could now sell them in branded packaging.

Once a product is branded, the manufacturer of that product is more interested in advertising its particular brand. For example, if a company made generic (unbranded) cookies, that company would have little interest in spending the money to advertise its cookies. By doing so, that cookie company would be helping its competitors in the cookie business, without receiving help from the other companies to pay for the advertising.

However, once a cookie company places its product in a box or bag with the company's name on it, the cookie company does benefit from advertising its products. This is because people will buy the particular brand of cookie they see advertised. In the 1800s, radio and television had not yet been invented. This means that most advertising was done in print media such as newspapers and magazines.

(continued)

Technology and Literacy: The 1800s -------------

3. Do you think manufacturers of cookies and other branded products wanted more people to be able to read or not? Explain your answer.

4. How did compulsory education benefit companies that advertised their products? Explain your answer.

The states that felt the least impact from the Industrial Revolution were southern states. This was partially due to the fact that these states still relied heavily on agriculture rather than manufacturing as a source of employment.

5. Do you think southern states were quick to enact compulsory education laws relative to northern states, or slower to enact these laws? Explain your answer.

6. In the late 1800s, do you think more people in the northern states could read than people in the southern states? Explain your answer.

Mechanical Reproduction and Visual Representation - - -

TECHNOLOGY HAS AN IMPACT on the number of people who can see a visual image. Today, an object can be photocopied, photographed, televised, webcast, or scanned. All of these media are examples of mechanical reproduction—using machinery to reproduce an image. Once the image is reproduced, one can "see" an object without having the object present. For example, many of us have never been to France to see Paris's Eiffel Tower. But most of us know what the tower looks like. Closer to home, not all Americans have been to the Statue of Liberty; but we know what the statue looks like.

Technology also has an impact on how we see things. For example, how do you know when it is 73 degrees outside? How do people who fish know where the fish are? How do blind people read? People use technology to learn about things that we cannot see with our eyes alone.

Timeline for Some of the Inventions that Change the Way We See	
1590	First modern microscope is invented by Zacharias Janssen (The Netherlands)
1607	First modern thermometer is invented by Galileo Galilei (Italy)
1609	First astronomical telescope is invented by Galileo Galilei (Italy)
1643	The barometer, which measures environmental air pressure, is invented by Evangelista Torricelli (Italy)
1769	First paper patterns of clothing developed by M. de Garsault (France)
1829	Braille type for the blind is invented by Louis Braille (France)
1888	First modern and relatively affordable camera is introduced by George Eastman (USA)
1891	Modern "movie" invented by Thomas Edison (USA)
1895	X-ray discovered by Wilhelm Roentgen (Germany)
1904	Radar is developed by Christian Hulsmeyer (Germany)
1916	First successful use of sonar by Paul Langevin and M. Chilowski (USA)
1926	Sound synchronization of movies developed by Warner Brothers Pictures (USA)
1938	Xerography, the basic method for photocopying, is invented by Chester F. Carlson (USA)
1947	The first instant camera is invented by Edwin Land (USA)

(continued)

Mechanical Reproduction and Visual Representation - - -

Suppose that Frosty Jane and Frosty Joe have been frozen in ice for the past five hundred years. Recently thawed out, our two chilly friends are curious about the ways people use different devices to see things. Jane and Joe are particularly curious about the following items. For each item they ask you about, describe what the item does (function) and why it is important (at least two uses). If you need more information, use library resources or the Internet.

Item	Function (what the item does)	Two Uses (why this item is important)
Microscope		
Barometer		
Paper Patterns for Clothing		
X-ray		
Radar		
Xerography		

Joe and Jane are impressed by your answers, but are not sure whether these types of devices are worth the expense. Select three of the types of visual devices listed above and explain how they can actually save money for some people or for most of society.

Item	Cost Savings Offered by Item
1.	
2.	
3.	

The Multinational Logo ------------------------------

A **LOGO** **IS** **A** **SYMBOL** that identifies a company. There are probably very few people in the world who do not recognize McDonald's golden arches. You also probably know which brand of computer uses an apple as its logo. Logos are an important substitute for words. A well-designed logo can help people quickly identify the company that is providing a good or a service. A good logo is also useful for multinational companies. Multinational companies are businesses that operate in several countries.

Wal-Mart, the American discount retailer, is an example of a multinational business. Wal-Mart currently has over 1,300 stores in 9 countries outside of the United States, including over 600 in Mexico, more than 90 in Germany, and over 46 stores in China and South Korea. Over the next few years, Wal-Mart plans to continue to add stores outside of the United States. Wal-Mart uses its logo on advertisements in television, magazines and news-papers, on its web sites, on its trucks, on its employees' uniforms, and on its store signs.

Record your answers below. Use another sheet of paper, if necessary.

1. Look at Wal-Mart's logo. What is one problem that Wal-Mart may face in Mexico and Germany?

2. Look again at Wal-Mart's logo. What is another problem that Wal-Mart may face in China and South Korea?

3. Suppose that you have been asked to create a new logo for Wal-Mart. Before you start designing this new logo, address each of the following issues:

   • Would you suggest that Wal-Mart consider changing the company's name or not? Explain your answer.

   • Suppose some people suggested that, because Wal-Mart is an American-based company, you include part or all of the American flag in your new logo. How would you reply? Explain your answer.

   • Should a new Wal-Mart logo be stylish and trendy, or should the new logo attempt to be a long-term, classic design? Explain your answer.

(continued)

The Multinational Logo –

- Should a new Wal-Mart logo use lots of different colors, or just a few? Explain your answer.

- Should a new Wal-Mart logo include just alphabetical lettering, just a symbol, or a combination of alphabetical lettering and a symbol? Explain your answer.

- What should a new logo identify about Wal-Mart? Does the logo need to refer to a characteristic of the company, such as offering low prices? Why or why not?

- Could the new logo be a "fanciful" design? For example, the Shell Oil Company's logo, suitably enough, is a seashell. However, few people associated a seashell with oil until Shell began using its name and logo. Other companies' logos are even more fanciful, resembling nothing found in nature. Should the new Wal-Mart logo use a "fanciful" design? Why or why not?

4. In the space below, draw your suggested logo for Wal-Mart:

5. Explain why you decided on this logo.

Design a Sign ---

THE PIECE OF PAPER that foreign visitors to the United States must fill out when arriving at an international airport or border crossing is called an I 94 form. This form is used to collect information about a visitor's identity, where the visitor is traveling within the United States, and what his or her purpose (business, pleasure, school) is for visiting the United States. Many countries ask visitors from the United States and other countries to fill out a similar form.

Several years ago, upon arriving at the international arrivals terminal in Boston, travelers saw a sign that read "Japanese I 94 forms." The sign was written just that way—in English, in our alphabet (which is based on the Latin alphabet). If a Japanese visitor does not read English, this sign is useless—Japanese have their own language and their own alphabet.

By yourself or in a group (as assigned by your teacher), create a sign that uses symbols instead of words to tell foreign visitors where they can find an I 94 form at the airport. Instead of different signs for different languages, create a sign that is universal. This means that your sign should contain symbols that can be reasonably understood by speakers of many different languages (for example, the doors of public restrooms often have signs with universal symbols). You will need to use another sheet of paper for your sign.

U.S. Department of Justice
Immigration and Naturalization Service

Welcome to the United States

36042779805

I-94 Arrival/Departure Record - Instructions

This form must be completed by all persons except U.S. Citizens, returning resident aliens, aliens with immigrant visas, and Canadian Citizens visiting or in transit.

Type or print legibly with pen in **ALL CAPITAL LETTERS**. Use English. Do not write on the back of this form.

This form is in two parts. Please complete both the Arrival Record (Item 1 through 13) and the Departure Record (Item 14 through 17).

When all items are completed, present this form to the U.S. Immigration and Naturalization Service Inspector.

Item 7 - If you are entering the United States by land, enter **LAND** in this space. If you are entering the United States by ship, enter **SEA** in this space.

Form I-94 (04-15-86)Y

Admission Number

36042779805

Immigration and
Naturalization Service
I-94
Arrival Record

1. Family Name
S M I T H
2. First (Given) Name
F R A N K
3. Birth Date (Day/Mo/Yr)
1 2 1 0 7 0
4. Country of citizenship
B R I T I S H
5. Sex (Male or Female)
M A L E
6. Passport number
5 4 3 8 9 0 0 1
7. Airline and Flight Number
B A 0 5
8. Country where you live
E N G L A N D
9. City Where You Boarded
L O N D O N
10. City Where Visa Was issued
L O N D O N
11. Date Issued (Day/Mo/Yr)
0 5 1 0 9 6
12 Address While in the United States (Number and Street)
9 0 9 S 5 T H S T R E E T
13. City and State
C H A M P A I G N I L

Departure Number

36042779805

Immigration and
Naturalization Service
I-94
Departure Record

14. Family Name
S M I T H
15. First (Given) Name
F R A N K
16. Birth Date (Day/Mo/Yr)
1 2 1 0 7 0
17. Country of citizenship
B R I T I S H

See Other Side   STAPLE HERE

An I 94 form

What Is Art? -

HUMAN BEINGS have produced and collected art from the time of cave people. We have discovered paintings, carvings, and other artifacts that are many thousands of years old.

Record your answers below. Use another sheet of paper, if necessary.

1. How can one tell the difference between a photograph that is meant as a document of something—a photograph of a new baby, a photograph of a sporting event, a photograph of a car accident—and a photograph that is meant to be considered as art? List and describe three differences between a documentary photograph and an artistic photograph.

   •

   •

   •

Fashion photography includes photographs of clothing and cosmetics that appear in magazines or newspapers. Famous fashion photographers are often paid large sums of money for their work.

2. Is fashion photography meant to be a document or art or both? Explain your answer.

Some paintings are representational—their subject matter represents something that can be seen in real life. For example, a portrait is meant to represent the person whose likeness is produced on canvas. A landscape painting may represent a city street or a painting of a mountain. Although a representational painting depicts something that is real, or at least could be real, it still possesses the painter's influence.

3. What makes a realistic painting more than just a document—what makes it a work of art? Explain your answer.

(continued)

What Is Art? -

Some paintings are abstract—they do not represent any object other than paint on canvas. For example, a blob of red paint and a smear of black paint on a white canvas may be considered art by some artists and art experts.

4. Why can a painting not be realistic and still be considered art? Explain your answer.

In July 1877, the art critic John Ruskin published an attack on a painting called *Nocturne in Black and Gold: The Falling Rocket.* This painting, by the American artist James McNeill Whistler, was on display in a London art gallery. Among other things, Ruskin accused Whistler of "flinging a pot of paint in the public's face." Whistler sued Ruskin in a British court for damaging his reputation. Whistler won the court case, but he was only awarded one farthing (the smallest British coin at the time—worth less than a penny). Although people's opinions varied at the time, many believed that neither Ruskin nor Whistler really won the case.

5. If a person does not like a painting or other work of art, should he or she be able to say or write anything he or she wants to about that work? Or should that person be careful to think about the artist's feelings and reputation? Explain your answer.

In 1999, New York's Brooklyn Art Museum displayed "The Holy Virgin Mary," by painter Chris Ofili. The painting included, among other items, several pieces of dried elephant dung attached to the canvas. Some people claimed that the painting was insulting to Christians; other people said that the painting was just plain ugly. The artist, a Catholic of African heritage living in Britain, said that the painting was not meant to be insulting to Christians. Instead, Ofili said that the use of the dung was an effort to combine his African heritage with European heritage. Rudolph Giuliani, New York City's mayor at the time, disliked the painting. Giuliani attempted to cut the city's financial support of the Brooklyn Art Museum because of the museum's display of the painting. A judge later ruled that Giuliani had wrongly interfered with the artist's and the museum's right to free speech when he tried to cut the museum's funding.

6. Can a painting, sculpture, or photograph be considered ugly or offensive by many people and still be considered a work of art? Explain why or why not.

"The Wall"—the Vietnam Veterans Memorial - - - - - - - - - -

VIETNAM IS A NATION in Southeast Asia. The United States was involved in a military conflict in Vietnam from the late 1950s until the middle 1970s. During this time, more than three million members of the American military served in Southeast Asia. Over 58,000 Americans were killed or declared missing during the conflict.

In 1980, the United States government gave land on the National Mall in Washington, D.C., to a veterans' group. This land was to be used to construct a memorial to those who served their country in Vietnam. In 1980, a veterans' group asked people to submit designs in a competition for the Memorial. Over 1,400 people entered the design competition. The competitors' names were not revealed to the judges. In 1981, a 21-year-old architecture student, Maya Ying Lin, was the surprise winner of the competition.

The winning proposal for the Memorial was greeted with shock by many people. Lin's design did not contain some of the more common features of war memorials, which often include sculptures of people and patriotic symbols. Instead, Lin placed a long, L-shaped black wall below the National Mall's lawn. The name of each American service member killed was etched in the wall. These names were arranged chronologically (by the date of each person's death) rather than alphabetically by name.

Despite the fact that Lin was born in Ohio, some observers were critical of the fact that Lin was of Asian heritage. Lin's parents had moved to the United States from China in 1949. Some people said that the Memorial should be designed by an "American." Many people said that only designs submitted by veterans of the Vietnam conflict should have been considered.

Record your answers below. Use another sheet of paper, if necessary.

1. Do you believe that some people who are born in the United States are more American (or less American) than other people born in the United States? Explain your answer.

2. Do you agree with the belief that only veterans should have been able to enter the competition to design the Memorial? Explain why or why not.

(continued)

"The Wall"—the Vietnam Veterans Memorial --------

3. Why do you think that the sponsors of the original design competition for the Memorial wanted to keep the names of the competitors hidden from the judges? Explain your answer.

4. Do you think that this was a good idea? Explain why or why not.

Some critics of Lin's design said the design needed to pay tribute not only to those service members who died in Vietnam, but to the millions of others who served there and survived. One of these critics was United States Secretary of Interior James Watt. Watt delayed the construction of Lin's design until the builders of the wall agreed to add other elements to the design. As a result, a sculpture, "Three Servicemen," was added a few yards from the wall. One of these men has Caucasian facial features, another African-American features, and the third has facial features that can be interpreted as either Hispanic American or Asian American. In 1993, another sculpture, the "Vietnam Women's Memorial," was added, honoring the more than 11,500 women who served in Vietnam.

5. Do you agree with the decision to add these sculptures to the original design? Explain why or why not.

Despite the criticism of the 1980s, the Vietnam Veterans Memorial has proved over more than two decades to be one of the most important memorials in the United States. More than four million people from different parts of the world visit the Memorial each year. Since the dedication of the Memorial in 1982, memorials of other American events now borrow features that Lin introduced for the first time in her design.

6. Why do you think the Vietnam Veterans Memorial, which was initially met with much hostility, has proved to be such an important symbol to so many people? Explain your answer.

The objectives of this unit are to help students

- recognize that even the most mundane of implements are the product of attitudes and values in addition to basic human needs
- understand the factors that enter into the design of buildings and spatial arrangements
- call on their creativity to generate material culture of their own

IN HIS BOOK *Material Culture in America,* cultural historian Thomas Schlereth tells us that, "[M]aterial culture can be considered to be the totality of artifacts in a culture, the vast universe of objects used by humankind to cope with the physical world, to facilitate social intercourse, to delight our fancy, and to create symbols of meaning . . ."[1] This unit focuses on the visual "things" that humans create. The impulse to create these things can be economic, social, political, or utilitarian. Students investigate a variety of common objects and places to develop a better understanding of the underlying motivation for their production.

[1] Schlereth, Thomas J., ed., *Material Culture Studies in America* (Nashville: American Association for State and Local History, 1982) p. 2.

In this Unit. . .

The Beetle and the Ram requires students to evaluate how carmakers incorporate design elements into their cars in order to appeal to specific gender groups. Students also suggest additional design elements that would be attractive to female and male motorists.

The Brake Light asks students to generate reasons in support of the 1985 federal regulation requiring a third, center brake light on new automobiles. Students also assess the government's efforts to make cars safer and the impact that safety features have on the cost of automobiles.

License Plates engages students in Internet research to collect information about their state or territory's official symbols and slogans. Students then integrate this information as they create a new license plate design of their own.

Bumper Stickers has students weigh the balancing of individual and societal interests with the exercise of free speech.

The Time Capsule asks students to identify important themes in contemporary American life and describe the everyday items that they would place in a time capsule to visually describe contemporary American life.

It's Fake, but It *Looks* Real has students investigate the human impulse to create artificial representations of natural items. Students also engage in Internet research to examine the American Plastics Council's efforts to generate goodwill for plastic goods.

Don't Judge a Book by Its Cover asks students to evaluate this adage and provide exceptions.

(continued)

Teacher Buzz (continued)

Money, Money, Money provides students with information about the ongoing redesign of American paper currency and the introduction of the euro in 2002. Students then identify the social and technological circumstances that underlie the designs of these currencies, and examine the possibility of moving toward digital currency.

The Shopping Mall has students visit a mall to explore how the architecture of the typical mall is designed to influence our behavior.

Mickey, the Silent Mouse provides students with the opportunity to assess the role that Mickey Mouse serves as an American icon.

How Do You Get There? has students investigate how people gather and use information to travel from one place to another. This activity sheet includes a group exercise that presents students with the challenge of drawing a map based on the oral instructions of a classmate.

EVERYTHING HUMANS CREATE—all the "stuff" we make—is made for a reason. Sometimes the reason is simple. For example, a cup or glass is made to drink from. However, there are thousands, if not millions, of different designs for cups. Many of these designs have very little to do with merely holding a liquid. Similarly, we build homes to provide shelter and security. Yet housing designs go far beyond merely putting a roof over people's heads.

> **"Everything humans create . . . is made for a reason."**

In this unit, we will look at some fairly ordinary items and places. Many of these are part of our everyday lives. We will move beyond thinking about the most obvious purpose for each of these items and places. Instead, we will study how items and places serve a number of less obvious needs and desires. Sometimes, those needs and desires are universal—common to all of us. At other times, different people have different needs and desires. We will see that occasionally the different meanings given to places and things can create conflict among different people.

Places and things, and the meanings that people give to them, are called "material culture." Many social scientists believe that a society's material culture tells important stories about that society. We will examine some of those stories in this unit.

The Beetle and the Ram ------------------------------

DO YOU KNOW people who refer to their cars as "he" or "she"? Cars can have gender distinctions. For example, trucks are frequently described as "tough" in their advertisements. This toughness is considered desirable by many males. When Volkswagen reintroduced the Volkswagen Beetle in 1997, it decided to advertise the car primarily to females. Unsurprisingly, then, most (but not all) trucks are purchased by males, and females are the most likely purchasers of the new Beetle.

Carmakers' efforts to appeal to a particular group of people go beyond just the way a car model is advertised. Car designers try to identify exterior **design elements** that appeal to certain groups of people. They then try to include these elements in their designs. For example, think about which current car models come with spoilers on the rear of the car. These spoilers' only function is visual appeal.

Record your answers below. Use another sheet of paper, if necessary.

1. Which type of driver do you think is attracted by a spoiler on a car?

Examine some of the exterior design elements of the Dodge Ram truck and the new Volkswagen Beetle, reintroduced in 1997. If you cannot find either vehicle on a street near you, visit the web sites for Dodge (dodge.com) and Volkswagen (vw.com).

2. Imagine you are visiting from another country and know nothing about the American advertising messages for the new Beetle. List two *exterior* design features of the Beetle that indicate that the car is targeted primarily toward females. Next to each item listed, explain why you think that item indicates an effort to appeal to females.

"Feminine" *Exterior* Feature	Explanation

3. Imagine you are visiting from another country and know nothing about the American advertising messages for the Dodge Ram. In the table that follows, list two *exterior* design features of the Dodge Ram that indicate that the vehicle is targeted primarily toward males. Next to each item listed, explain why you think that item indicates an effort to appeal to males.

(continued)

The Beetle and the Ram -

"Masculine" *Exterior* Feature	Explanation

4. Now, imagine you are a designer for Volkswagen, and you want to add at least two *interior* features to make the new Beetle even more attractive to female drivers. (They can be anything you want to add, as long as they would appeal to females.) What two features will you add? Explain your reasons for each feature.

"Feminine" *Interior* Feature	Explanation

5. Imagine that you are a designer for Dodge, and you want to add at least two *interior* features to make the Dodge Ram even more attractive to male drivers. (Again, they can be anything you want, as long as they appeal to males.) What two features will you add? Explain your reasons for each feature.

"Masculine" *Interior* Feature	Explanation

The Brake Light -

IN THE 1970s, most automobiles had two back lights that glowed red when the driver applied the automobile's brakes. During this time, a psychologist, John Voevodsky, studied how people responded to two brake lights. He compared those responses to how people behaved when they saw three brake lights. The third brake light was mounted in the center and higher than the other brake lights on the back of cars. Voevodsky found that people reacted more quickly to the new set of three lights than they did to the traditional two lights.

As the result of Voevodsky's research, a federal law went into effect in 1985. This law required a third, higher mounted brake light to be placed on the center of the rear of all automobiles beginning with the 1986 model year. The U.S. government enacted this law hoping that the new regulation would help prevent accidents and injuries. The government has been pleased with the results of the 1985 law. A 1998 study concluded that center brake lights help prevent over ninety thousand crashes and more than fifty thousand injuries each year.

Record your answers below. Use another sheet of paper, if necessary.

1. Consider how people's eyes and minds work. Then list and describe three reasons why you think the third, higher mounted center brake light on the back of cars has helped prevent car accidents.

    •

    •

    •

Traffic experts found that the third brake light makes cars safer. Over the years, the U.S. government has also enacted regulations requiring airbags in new cars, as well as improved seatbelts, stronger bumpers, and other items that make cars safer to drive. However, safety often costs money. When automobile manufacturers are required to add these safety features, they pass the expense of adding those features on to the consumers who buy those cars.

(continued)

The Brake Light ----------------------------------

2. The 1998 government study estimated that the third brake lights save $3.18 in prop-
   erty damage for every $1 that they cost. Of course, every person buying a new car
   after 1985 had to pay for the third brake light, even though most drivers are not
   involved in accidents. Do you believe that the money saved justifies the cost of the
   light? Explain why or why not.

3. Some people are worried that if the federal government continues to require more
   safety features on cars, that fewer and fewer people will be able to afford a new car.
   • Why do you think they say this?

   • Do you agree? Explain why or why not.

4. Suppose some people are only able to afford an older used car that lacks the safety
   features required in a new car. Should the government require those people to add
   the new safety features to the car at their own expense? Explain why or why not.

5. Do you think the government should be able to require all people to buy cars with
   certain safety features even if some people do not want them? Or do you think a
   consumer should be given the choice to decide which safety features he or she wants
   or does not want to pay for? Explain your answer.

License Plates -

THE STANDARD AUTOMOBILE license plate in the United States is twelve inches wide by six inches tall. Until fairly recently, most states' license plates were pretty simple looking. They were usually printed in only two colors, one for the background and one for the lettering. The license plate had little information other than the state's name and the license plate number. Occasionally, a state might have added a slogan, such as Idaho's "Famous Potatoes" or Louisiana's "Sportsman's Paradise." The trend within the last twenty years or so, however, is to add much more color and design elements to license plates. Many states also offer motorists a choice of different types of specialty plates. These include hobbies. For example, Texas has a license plate that celebrates hunting. A specialty plate may be devoted to a particular college or university. Maryland has plates for alumni of several schools, including Penn State—a non-Maryland school. Many states have plates that commemorate motorists' service in the different military branches.

Record your answers below. Use another sheet of paper, if necessary.

1. Why do you think the states have begun to add more color and design elements to their license plates than they had just a few years ago? Explain your answer.

Imagine you have been asked to design a new license plate for your state (or, depending where you live, your territory or district). This license plate is intended to be for general usage, rather than as a specialty plate. You will draw your new plate in the space on the following page. Before you begin drawing, think about and respond to the following questions.

2. Visit the "50 States" web site on the Internet (50states.com). Then click on your state's name. Find the following information. If you live in a district or territory, you can search for this information on the Internet using a search engine, such as Google (google.com) or Excite (excite.com).

   • What is your state's official bird?

   • What is your state's official tree?

   • What is your state's official flower?

   • What is your state's official slogan?

   • What is your state's official nickname?

(continued)

License Plates -

3. Does your state currently use any of the preceding items on its license plates? Explain.

4. Will you use any of the preceding items on the license plate that you will design? Explain why or why not.

Some states have various pictures of wildlife or scenery that are common in that state. These pictures may include official wildlife of a state, but many states use other pictures as well. For example, Utah's license plate includes an illustration of the Delicate Arch desert stone formation. Some states use a distinctive symbol, such as the Native American Zia sun symbol that appears on New Mexico's license plate.

5. What symbols or designs will you have on the license plate? Describe it and provide your reason for using it. (If your state's license plate already has a distinctive symbol or design, create a new one that is appropriate.)

6. The colors of some state license plates are the same as the color of those states' flags. However, this is not always the case. What colors will you use on your state's license plate? Explain why.

7. In the space below, draw your design for a new license plate for your state.

Looking for more information about license plates? Visit worldlicenseplates.com. This is a web site created for collectors of license plates.

Bumper Stickers -

THE UNITED STATES SUPREME COURT decided the case of *Wooley v. Maynard* in 1977. The Court ruled that New Hampshire residents George and Maxine Maynard could legally cover up part of their automobile's license plate. The Maynards were not allowed to cover up the numbers and letters that are used to identify an automobile. However, they were allowed to cover up New Hampshire's official state motto, which appears on the state's license plates. That motto is, "Live Free or Die." Mr. Maynard said that he covered up the state motto because it contradicted his family's religious beliefs. Maynard told that court that he refused "to be [forced] by the State into advertising a slogan which I find morally, ethically, religiously and politically [objectionable]."

The Supreme Court said that the Maynards' right to cover up the state motto was protected by the United States Constitution's First Amendment. The Court said

> "The fact that most individuals agree with the thrust of New
> Hampshire's motto is not the test. . . . The First Amendment protects the
> right of individuals to hold a point of view different from the majority
> and to refuse to foster, in the way New Hampshire commands, an idea
> they find morally objectionable."

Record your answers below. Use another sheet of paper, if necessary.

1. Do you agree that people should be able to cover up a state motto or other saying on a license plate if they disagree with the message of that motto or saying? Explain why or why not.

The nine members of the Supreme Court were not unanimous in this decision. Three members of the Court dissented to (disagreed with) the majority's decision. They believed that the Maynards should not be able to cover up any part of a state's license plate. Instead, they said that the Maynards could have placed a bumper sticker next to the license plate telling people that they disagreed with what the license plate said.

2. Regardless of how you answered question 1, do you think this bumper sticker suggestion is a good one or not? Explain your answer.

(continued)

Bumper Stickers —

The First Amendment of the United States Constitution protects freedom of speech. However, not all speech is protected. For example, the United States Supreme Court has ruled that words that could start a fight or words that create a clear and present danger are not protected by the First Amendment.

In 1975, another court considered a case in which a Mississippi school district had fired a teacher. One of the reasons for the firing was because the teacher regularly drove to school in a car with a bumper sticker that said, "If at first you don't succeed, try a-gun."

3. Do you think the teacher's bumper sticker should be protected by the First Amendment? Explain why or why not.

In criminal and civil court trials, the judge is responsible for deciding whether or not people are qualified to serve as jurors in the trial. In some communities, judges ask potential jurors if they have any bumper stickers on their automobile, and if so, what those bumper stickers say.

4. Why do you think judges want to know about the types of bumper stickers that potential jurors place on their automobiles? Explain your answer.

In some parts of the world, tourists are more likely to be the victims of robbery than other people. Because of this problem, there has been some discussion over whether or not car rental companies should place bumper stickers that advertise the companies' names on their rental cars.

5. Do you believe that there should be a law that prohibits rental car companies from placing bumper stickers that advertise the companies' names on the companies' rental vehicles? Explain your answer.

The Time Capsule -

AS WE SAID in the introduction to this unit, one of the ways we study a society is by examining its "material culture." Material culture is a type of visual culture, which is the subject of this book. Material culture is the "stuff" we use in everyday life that helps tell the story of our lives. This story has different **themes.** There are many themes occurring at the same time. Some themes are long lasting, while some are short-lived.

Some of these themes are visualized by the use of **icons.** One of the most famous American icons is the Statute of Liberty. There should be no mystery about what American theme she represents!

One of the most famous advertising icons was the Marlboro Man. The Marlboro Man, an unnamed cowboy on a horse riding along through rugged terrain, helped to sell a lot of cigarettes over several decades. He was seen as more than merely a smoker. The Marlboro Man was a popular icon because his image represented the themes of American ruggedness and independence.

Today, the cell phone is an icon that represents different themes to different people. For many teenagers, it represents freedom and independence. It also represents friendships and fun. For older adults, the cell phone often represents responsibility. This responsibility may be tied to work (talking to the boss or a customer) or it may be tied to home (talking to a spouse or a child).

Record your answers below. Use another sheet of paper, if necessary.

Imagine you have been asked by the U.S. government to collect items for placement in a time capsule. The purpose of the time capsule is to use our current material culture to explain significant themes in the United States during the year. This time capsule will be opened one hundred years from now. You should try to identify items that explain the "big picture," rather than what happens to be popular among just a small group of your friends at the time. You should also try to identify items that represent important activities and events that are happening today. For example, a flag is an icon of America. However, it has been so for hundreds of years, and would not be helpful in describing the current times. In addition, you should try to identify items that are identified with American life in particular, not life everywhere.

In the table on the following page, list five items that you will place in the time capsule. (You may not use a cell phone, since it has already been discussed.) Provide an explanation for each of your choices by discussing which theme(s) of American life it represents. Suggestion: If you are having trouble identifying five items, think first about important themes. Then try to identify items that represent those themes.

(continued)

The Time Capsule -

Item	Theme(s) the Item Represents
1.	
2.	
3.	
4.	
5.	

It's Fake, but It *Looks* Real -

YOU ARE CERTAINLY AWARE that there are differences between what is natural and what is made by people. Often, items that people make are referred to as fake or artificial. Today, you will often see an artificial item, such as an artificial pearl, referred to as *faux* (pronounced *foe*). This is simply the French word for *fake,* but it sounds fancier.

Record your answers below. Use another sheet of paper, if necessary.

Sometimes, artificial items contain none of the substance that is being imitated. For example, many products come with plastic wood-grain decals or panels to make them look like wood. At other times, an item made by humans is not completely artificial, but has been somehow "engineered." Laboratory-created gems are an example of an engineered item. They are not viewed by jewelry experts as artificial, but they are not considered natural, either. Perhaps plywood also falls into this category. It is made mostly of wood, but it has been manufactured by people using pieces of real wood and glue.

1. Look around your classroom or your home and find some uses of artificial wood.

   • What characteristics of wood do humans like?

   • Why do we find wood furnishings (or wood-looking) furnishings comforting?

2. In addition to artificial wood, find two other examples of artificial products used to furnish schools or homes, and list them here.

(continued)

It's Fake, but It *Looks* Real -

People often consider artificial items to be "cheap" or not as good as a natural item. Because of this, we typically expect an artificial item to cost less than the natural item. In fact, this is often the reason why people create artificial items—as a less expensive substitute for natural products. However, this is not always the case. Artificial sweeteners cost more per pound than sugar does.

3. List another artificial item that is often more expensive than the natural item it replaces.

4. Explain why this item costs more than a natural item.

Things that are artificial, or that appear artificial, are sometimes negatively referred to as "plastic." Similarly, insincere people are often called plastic. Visit the American Plastics Council's web site, plastics.org. Browse the site for a while, and click on some of the links.

5. Describe how the Council attempts to overcome the perception of plastic as some-thing that is cheap by providing three examples from the web site below. Explain each example.

    •

    •

    •

6. Did the Council's web site change your view of plastic? Explain why or why not.

7. Imagine you have ordered a piece of furniture that you thought was wood. When it arrives, you discover that it is metal, and plastic stickers that look like wood have been included in the package. Would you place the plastic stickers on the piece of furniture? Why or why not?

Don't Judge a Book by Its Cover ------------------

YOU HAVE PROBABLY HEARD the expression, "Don't judge a book by its cover."

Record your answers below. Use another sheet of paper, if necessary.

1. Explain what the expression above means.

2. Do you believe that most people you know follow this advice? Explain why or why not.

3. Do you believe this is good advice or bad advice? Explain why.

4. Provide three examples of situations that support your view, as explained in question 3. Describe each example.

5. There are exceptions to nearly every rule. Describe one exception to your viewpoint.

Money, Money, Money -

IN 1996, the United States Bureau of Engraving and Printing, the government agency that prints banknotes (paper money or "bills"), introduced significant changes in the design of the nation's banknotes. That year, new designs for the $100, $50, $20, $10, and $5 bills were introduced. Although these were the first significant changes in the design of banknotes in over sixty-seven years, the Bureau also announced that it would begin to make regular design changes to the bills on a 7- to 10-year cycle. Thus, in October 2003, the Bureau began a new round of new designs, starting with the $20 bill. These latest changes include the use of a pale shade of peach on the $20 banknote, in addition to the standard green hues. New $50 bills are to be introduced in 2004, and new $100 bills in 2005.

Record your answers below. Use another sheet of paper, if necessary.

1. Why do you think the Bureau of Engraving and Printing has decided to change the design of American banknotes more frequently than it has in the past? Explain your answer.

2. Why do you think the Bureau decided not to change the design of the $1 bill in 1996, although the Bureau changed all of the other bills' designs? Explain your answer.

3. Why do you think that the Bureau decided to change the design of the $20 bill in 2003, before changing the designs of the other denominations? Explain your answer.

(continued)

Money, Money, Money--------------------------------

The symbol for the euro

In January 2002, twelve European countries stopped using their own currencies and began using the euro, a common currency shared by those countries. One of the considerations when the new money was being designed was the fact that there are several different languages spoken in the countries that now use the euro. These languages include French, Greek, German, Finnish, English, and Dutch.

The front of each euro banknote features an illustration of a doorway. The back of each euro banknote features an illustration of a bridge. (The doorway and bridge is different for each banknote, depending on its denomination.)

4. Why do you think the designers of the euro banknotes chose to use drawings of doorways and bridges? Explain your answer.

American banknotes and coins feature the likenesses of former American presidents and political leaders, including Abraham Lincoln on the penny and the five dollar bill, and George Washington on the quarter and one dollar bill. As mentioned, the new euro banknotes feature illustrations of doorways and bridges. The new euro coins feature engravings of maps of Europe on the front of each coin. Each of the twelve countries using the euro coins has their own designs for the back of the coins.

5. Why do you think that the euro banknotes and coins do not contain illustrations of people? Explain your answer.

(continued)

Money, Money, Money-------------------------------

Some people have questioned whether we need paper currency at all in today's world. They suggest that plastic cards with magnetic stripes could be used instead. These cards, similar in appearance to credit cards, would have data on the magnetic stripe. This data would tell how much value was on the card. When paying for something, the cardholder would present it to the other person, who would swipe the card in an electronic reader. By this process, funds would be electronically shifted from one person's account to another. When the card's value got too low, the cardholder could replenish its value by taking it to a machine similar to an Automatic Teller Machine (ATM). Or the cardholder could use the Internet to replenish the card's value.

6. What would be one *advantage* of substituting electronic data cards for paper banknotes? Explain your answer.

7. What would be one *disadvantage* of substituting electronic data cards for paper banknotes? Explain your answer.

8. Do you believe that electronic data cards may someday replace paper banknotes? Explain why or why not.

The Shopping Mall -

ARCHITECTS DESIGN BUILDINGS. Some architects use so-called "psychological architecture" techniques when designing buildings such as gambling casinos. They use these techniques to help influence the behavior of their customers. This is because casino owners want to encourage gamblers to spend as much money as possible. The entrance to a casino is very easy to find. The exit from a casino is usually not so easily found. Casinos rarely have any windows. Casinos never have any clocks visible to their customers. Casinos also require that people walk past the gambling machines and tables to get to other facilities, such as restrooms or places to eat.

Psychological architecture techniques are also used in the design of shopping malls. The purpose of shopping-mall architecture is similar to that of casinos: to encourage people to spend their money. This activity requires that you visit a mall and answer the following questions.

Record your answers below. Use another sheet of paper, if necessary.

1. As you approach a mall, how do you know where the entrance to the mall is?

   • As you leave a mall, how do you know where the exit is?

   • Which is easier to find—the entrance or the exit? Explain your answer.

   • Why do you think there are such differences in the design of the entrance into a mall and the design of the exit?

2. Watch some other people as they enter the mall—which direction do most of them turn—right or left?

   • Why do you think this is so?

3. How many clocks did you see inside the mall?

   • Where were those clocks?

(continued)

The Shopping Mall ----------------------------------

- Explain why you think the architect decided on this number and location of the clocks.

4. Where are the restrooms in the mall? Are they clearly marked and easy to get to, or are they out of the way?

- Why do you think restrooms are located in this manner? Explain your answer.

5. Hamburgers and pizza are some of our favorite fast foods. Are there several choices of hamburgers and pizza in the mall's food court, or are the choices limited? Explain why you think this is the case.

6. Stores that specialize in women's clothing usually do not want to be located near the food court. Explain why you think this is so.

7. Casinos often prefer that their customers use plastic colored chips instead of cash. Similarly, stores at the mall often ask customers if they would like to charge their purchases on a credit card instead of using cash. Why do you think that casinos and shopping malls both want their customers to use substitutes for cash rather than cash? Explain your answer.

8. Some people say that the shopping mall is an icon of America. This means that the shopping mall symbolizes America. Do you agree or disagree? Explain your answer.

Mickey, the Silent Mouse –

MICKEY MOUSE made his first appearance in Walt Disney's movie cartoon, "Steamboat Willie" in 1928. For many years, Mickey was an active, speaking character in countless Disney film cartoons and in Disney comic books. Today, however, Mickey is often a silent figure. Some people say that Mickey is no longer a character; he is now an icon of the Walt Disney Company. In fact, Andy Mooney, the chairman of Disney Consumer Products division in 2003, has said that Mickey is "our swoosh," comparing Mickey's face to the famous Nike logo. (In fact, Mooney came to Disney after working at Nike.) Although Mickey still occasionally appears as a speaking character, he has not appeared in a Disney video since 1995. Nevertheless, Mickey's face can be seen on clothing, toothbrushes, coffee mugs, key chains, and other consumer products sold by Disney. Disney's Consumer Products division has sales of nearly $400 million a year. Mickey remains the most popular Disney character, accounting for approximately forty percent of the company's merchandise sales.

Record your answers below. Use another sheet of paper, if necessary.

1. Dennis Green, Disney's Vice President for Apparel in 2003, has said that, "Mickey has always been cool." Do you agree? Explain why or why not.

2. Why do you think children want Disney merchandise? Explain your answer.

3. Why do you think adults buy Disney merchandise for themselves? Explain your answer.

4. Some people say that Mickey Mouse is much more powerful as a silent icon than as a speaking character. Why do you think they say this?

   • Do you agree? Explain why or why not.

5. Will the American public ever grow tired of Mickey Mouse? Explain why or why not.

How Do You Get There? -

MOST MAPS are ornithological—this means that they are seen from a bird's eye view of the area mapped. Studies have found that males tend to look quickly at landmarks (a building, a sign) as they begin their journey. Males often use a sense of direction based on "survey representation." This means that males often use an ornithological view for imagining a journey. Females are more likely to try to picture the entire route in their head, and then follow that mental map. Females often use a "route representation" or street level method for direction, based on left, right, down a hill, up a hill, and so forth.

Some scientists believe that these gender differences originate from the days when most humans were hunters and gatherers. Males often traveled far from home to hunt animals, while females tended to stay closer to home as they gathered edible vegetation. Since males would often find themselves in new surroundings as they hunted, they relied on remembering certain landmarks (a tree, a stream) in the new landscape to find their way home. Females would routinely visit the same areas, so they found their way home based on a mental map of the places they had been to many times before.

In modern society, few of us are still hunters and gatherers. Thus, these gender differences should be less obvious today than they were years ago. However, different people visualize a route in different ways.

Record your answers below. Use another sheet of paper, if necessary.

1. This exercise should be done in groups of two. Find a classmate who does not know where you live, and vice versa. If possible, find a classmate of the opposite gender—a female should team up with a male, and vice versa. Orally describe to that classmate how you travel from home to school. While you describe your route, your classmate should draw a map that represents your description of your route home. Do not look at your classmate's map while describing your route! Then change roles—have your classmate describe their route home, while you try to map it. Again, do not allow your classmate to look at your map while he or she is describing the route.

   • After completing both maps, review each other's map. Describe how accurate each map was.

(continued)

How Do You Get There? -

Suppose you have just arrived at a train station in a large city in Notmycountry. You are unable to find anyone there who speaks your language, and you do not speak Notmycountryese, the language of Notmycountry. You have decided to stay in a small inn that a friend told you about. Your friend says the inn is within reasonable walking distance, heading north, from the train station. Unfortunately, your friend could not remember the name of the inn, nor its address.

2. If you could select *only one* of the following three items, which do you think would be the most useful for helping you find your way to the inn? Explain why.

   - A map of the city
   - A book with translations of common Notmycountryese and English words and phrases
   - A compass

3. Which of the three items above do you think would be the least useful to you? Explain why.

The objectives of this unit are to help students

- understand the competing social and economic forces that influence the media, and vice versa
- recognize that the media influence how people perceive reality
- anticipate the technological changes that will affect the media in the future

STUDENTS ARE heavy consumers of commercial media. Because the media's role is primarily to entertain, students will often resist engaging in critical thinking about the media. However, students' consumption of media also makes them experts of a sort. This sense of expertise assists students in this unit's discussions of our relationship with the media.

In this Unit. . .

Are Billboards Good or Bad? has students compare arguments that support the presence of billboards along roadways and arguments that oppose billboards. Students also generate an additional argument for each position. They then evaluate both sides of the argument and discuss which is more persuasive.

What Is the Future of Magazines and Newspapers? asks students to weigh the comparative advantages and disadvantages of the media's move away from paper and ink toward digital technology.

What Is the Future of All Print Media? offers students the opportunity to predict the social and economic impact of technology in the future.

The White Van provides students with information about the repeated erroneous sightings of a white van during the Beltway sniper shootings of October 2002. Students use this information to assess the media's ability to influence what

we see. They also investigate "false memory syndrome" and the relationship between truth and memory. You may wish to include Hans Christian Andersen's classic story "The Emperor's New Suit" to discuss popular opinion's effect on individuals' perception.

The Rodney King Beating has students examine whether the repeated viewing of violent images desensitizes viewers to violence. Students also assess how the race of the viewer influences his or her perception of different racial groups.

Cinema Therapy introduces students to the use of movies to help people deal with important issues in their lives. Students identify movies they would recommend to friends involved in a variety of personal situations, and describe why those movies would be appropriate for each situation.

The Written Word Versus the Oral Word has students explore the relationship between visual media and individual learning styles.

Video Games uses a discussion of this popular entertainment medium to engage students in an investigation of the potential educational applications of video games. In addition, students are asked to evaluate how individual learning styles affect the acquisition of gaming skills and knowledge. Students are also encouraged to use their creativity as they propose a new video game of their own.

HOMES BUILT in the United States in the early part of the twentieth century often had only one pair of electric sockets in each room. Today, building laws often require an electric socket to be placed along every six feet of wall. Many of us now have rooms with six or more sets of electric sockets. One of the primary reasons for the demand for more electricity is the use of televisions, videocassette recorders (VCRs), DVD players, video games, and home theater systems. Ninety-eight percent of American homes have a television. Of course, many homes have more than one television. Nearly every adult American who wants a television has one.

> **"The popular demand for visual media seems always to be increasing."**

Twenty years ago, the introduction of the VCR frightened movie theater owners. The theater owners thought that the presence of VCRs in people's homes would hurt the theater business. However, movie theaters have since enjoyed record attendance. It is now thought that video and DVD movies actually help movie theaters instead of hurt them. The belief is that home movie viewing "primes the pump" for theaters. This means that people's interest in movies is increased by watching movies at home. Home movie watching may actually encourage people to visit movie theaters more often.

The popular demand for visual media seems always to be increasing. For example, many of the early television broadcasts of sporting events in the 1940s used only one camera. Instant replay did not exist. Today, the contract between the National Football League (NFL) and television broadcasters requires that all football games have a minimum of seven television cameras and five videotape machines. For its Monday Night Football telecasts, ABC often uses more than two dozen cameras, including one in a blimp. The NFL realizes that it must compete with other forms of entertainment. Thus, the NFL relies heavily on visual media to attract viewers.

Not all visual media are electronic. We are also exposed to newspapers, magazines, billboards, and other forms of nonelectronic media. However, we will see in this unit that the current expansion of computing and digital technology may eventually cause many nonelectronic media to vanish in the future.

Are Billboards Good or Bad? —

THE UNITED STATES SUPREME COURT has ruled that commercial speech is protected by the First Amendment of the United States Constitution. However, the Court has also said that commercial speech does not enjoy the same degree of protection as ideological speech. (Ideological speech includes religious and political speech.) So, while the government cannot prohibit all forms of commercial speech, it can impose reasonable time, place, and manner restrictions on commercial speech.

Record your answers below. Use another sheet of paper, if necessary.

Billboards are a form of commercial speech. Over the years, there has been debate about how to balance the interests of the billboard industry and the interests of those who oppose billboards. Both sides of this debate offer several persuasive arguments to support their views.

Arguments *Supporting* Billboards	Arguments *Opposing* Billboards
a. Billboard rental provides money for the landowners who rent space to billboard companies. b. Billboards help the economy and provide jobs for people. This includes the people who work for the billboard industry, as well as the people who work for the companies that advertise on billboards. c. Billboards inform motorists about new jobs, coming events, and other practical information. According to a 1997 survey, 76 percent of Americans say billboards provide useful information.[1] d. Billboards help tourists. According to a 1991 survey, 93 percent of automobile travelers in America rely on billboards to locate gas, food, lodging, and tourist attractions.[2] e. There are many more important issues facing our government leaders. They should not be worrying about regulating billboards.	a. Billboards are unattractive. b. Billboards obstruct travelers' views of scenic areas. c. Billboards are a dangerous distraction to motorists. There is a high correlation between the presence of billboards and traffic accidents.[3] d. The billboard industry is not comprised of small businesspeople. It is dominated by three multibillion-dollar conglomerates.[4] e. Private citizens opposed to billboards must compete with the huge corporations that pay large salaries to public relations firms and government relations firms, which use their power to influence political leaders. f. The billboard industry tries to manipulate public opinion with its occasional donations of free or discounted signs to charitable organizations.

(continued)

Are Billboards Good or Bad? -

Arguments *Supporting* Billboards	Arguments *Opposing* Billboards
f. The billboard industry is very generous in contributing free or discounted signs to charities and other important causes. g. (your argument) _____ _____ _____ _____ [1] Penn, Schoen & Berland—1997 (a national poll conducted for the Outdoor Advertising Association of America). [2] U.S. Travel Data Center—1991.	g. (your argument) _____ _____ _____ _____ [3] Federal Highway Administration Commercial Electronic Variable-Message Signage (CEVMS) Report, 1980. [4] Clear Channel Communications, Inc.; Viacom, Inc.; and Lamar Advertising Company.

1. These are not all of the arguments for either side of the debate. Think of another argument in support of billboards and fill in line g in the "Supporting" column above. Explain your answer.

2. Think of another argument in opposition to billboards and fill in line g in the "Opposing" column above. Explain your answer.

3. Review the seven arguments (the six listed on page 45 and above and the one you have added) in the "Supporting" column. Which argument is the *most* persuasive? Explain why.

(continued)

Are Billboards Good or Bad? -

4. Review the seven arguments (the six listed on page 45 and above and the one you have added) in the "Supporting" column. Which argument is the *least* persuasive? Explain why.

5. Review the seven arguments (the six listed on page 45 and the one you have added) in the "Opposing" column. Which argument is the *most* persuasive? Explain why.

6. Review the seven arguments (the six listed on page 45 and the one you have added) in the "Opposing" column. Which argument is the *least* persuasive? Explain why.

7. Considering all of the arguments supporting billboards and the arguments opposing billboards, do you personally support billboards or do you oppose them? Explain your answer.

What Is the Future of Magazines and Newspapers? - - - -

YOU MAY HAVE SEEN episodes of the old cartoon *The Jetsons.* The Jetson family, a mythical family of the future, zooms around in rocket-powered cars, has a robot for a maid, and swallows instantly dispensed pills instead of preparing and eating regular meals. Maybe it would be fun to have a rocket-powered car and convenient to have a robotic maid. But would you really rather take a pill instead of eating a delicious meal? Just because technology can create something does not mean that people will accept it.

The technology needed to produce a paper-thin electronic tablet that could replace the traditional paper-based magazine or newspaper is rapidly becoming available. A new computer with a monitor will be no thicker or heavier than a current printed-on-paper magazine. Although this technology is currently very expensive, it will become affordable for many readers. Instead of readers having to buy a paper copy of a newspaper or a magazine, those publications will be available through wireless Internet connections. A reader can use the same device to read as many publications as he or she cares to. Some electronic publications may be free (with advertisers paying for the cost of publication). Others may charge for a single issue or a monthly/annual subscription, just as they do today.

Record your answers below. Use another sheet of paper, if necessary.

Think about readers of magazines. Many magazine readers are interested in the thoughtful articles or attractive photographs in magazines.

1. What would be an *advantage* for readers if electronic versions of magazines replace paper versions? Explain your answer.

2. What would be a *disadvantage* for readers if electronic versions of magazines replace paper versions? Explain your answer.

3. Do you think readers will eventually prefer an electronic version of magazines to paper versions? Explain why or why not.

(continued)

What Is the Future of Magazines and Newspapers? - - - -

Now consider the readers of newspapers. Newspaper readers often seek the latest news and other information.

4. What would be an *advantage* for readers if electronic versions of newspapers replace paper versions? Explain your answer.

5. What would be a *disadvantage* for readers if electronic versions of newspapers replace paper versions? Explain your answer.

6. Do you think readers will eventually prefer an electronic version of newspapers to paper versions? Explain why or why not.

Advertisers help to keep down the price of magazines and newspapers. This is because most of a magazine's or a newspaper's profit comes from advertisements.

Let us consider advertisers.

7. What would be an *advantage* for advertisers if electronic versions of magazines and newspapers replace paper versions? Explain your answer.

8. What would be a *disadvantage* for advertisers if electronic versions of magazines and newspapers replace paper versions? Explain your answer.

9. Do you think advertisers will eventually prefer an electronic version of magazines and newspapers to paper versions? Explain why or why not.

What Is the Future of All Print Media? - - - - - - - - - - - - - - -

A FEW YEARS AGO, the computer software manufacturer Microsoft made the following predictions:

- In the year 2009, electronic book titles will begin to outsell paper in many categories. Title prices are lower, but sales are higher.

- In 2010, electronic book devices will weigh half a pound, run twenty-four hours, and hold as many as a million titles.

- In 2018, major newspapers will publish their last paper editions and move solely to electronic distribution.

- In 2019, paper books remain popular as gifts, for collectors, for books of fine art and photography, and for those who prefer a print-reading experience.

- In 2020, ninety percent of all titles are sold in electronic as well as paper form. Webster's dictionary alters its first definition of the word "book." The new definition for "book" is "a substantial piece of writing commonly displayed on a computer or other personal viewing device."

Record your answers below. Use another sheet of paper, if necessary.

1. Do you agree with Microsoft's predictions? Explain why or why not.

2. If printed books are wanted by a smaller group of readers in 2019 than today, and are sought largely by collectors and gift givers, do you think that printed books will become more expensive or less expensive? Explain your answer.

As technology changes the way we receive information, people face the possibility of losing their jobs due to "technological unemployment." Technological unemployment is the result of technology replacing or eliminating processes used to create products. For example, fewer people are needed to make a product when machinery replaces some people in the assembly process. Technological unemployment is also created when technology replaces or eliminates products themselves. For example, there are very few manufacturers of typewriters today. This is because fewer and fewer people are using typewriters.

(continued)

What Is the Future of All Print Media? – – – – – – – – – – – – –

3. Identify three types of businesses whose employees may have their jobs threatened if electronic media replace printed reading material.

Technology does not just create unemployment; it also creates new employment opportunities. For example, when the automobile began to replace the horse as the primary means of transportation, many people who tended horses lost their jobs. However, automobile manufacturers employ millions of people today.

4. Identify three types of businesses that may hire new employees if electronic media replace printing of reading material.

5. Predict the future of a school or community library. List three ways that a library in the year 2020 will differ from the library of today. Explain each of your answers.

   •

   •

   •

6. Predict the future of a school or community library in the year 2100. Will libraries still exist? Explain why or why not.

The White Van ---------------------------------------

IN OCTOBER 2002, people living in Washington, D.C., and surrounding areas in Virginia and Maryland were terrorized by the so-called Beltway sniper. Between October 2 and October 23, ten people were killed and three others injured in apparently random shootings. The press began to report that witnesses to some of these shootings described seeing a white box truck or a white van nearby. Few details about the white truck or van were provided. Police from different law-enforcement agencies throughout the area conducted roadblocks. The roadblocks stopped numerous white trucks and white vans in the search for suspects.

One woman later testified that she thought she saw a suspicious dark blue car near one of the shootings. Yet she did not notify police, because she had heard on television and read in the newspapers that police were looking for a white van, not a blue car. On October 24, 2002, John Allen Muhammad and Lee Boyd Malvo were arrested in a 1990 dark blue Chevrolet Caprice. Found inside the car was the rifle that was used in the killings. No more sniper-related shootings have been reported in the Washington area since Muhammad and Malvo were arrested. In November 2003, after a trial, Muhammad was convicted of murder and sentenced to death. Malvo's trial began shortly afterward, and he was convicted and sent to prison.

Record your answers below. Use another sheet of paper, if necessary.

1. When a serious crime occurs, police usually ask witnesses to the crime to report what they have seen. The police often rely on the news media to ask any unknown witnesses to come forward and provide information. Are eyewitnesses always reliable? Explain why or why not.

2. Do you believe that the news media affect our way of seeing things? Explain why or why not.

3. You have probably heard the saying, "Seeing is believing." Is this saying true? Explain why or why not.

(continued)

The White Van -------------------------------

4. Some psychologists and lawyers talk about "false memory syndrome." They say people can be made to believe they saw something they did not actually see. Do you believe that otherwise reasonable people can be made to believe they saw something they did not actually see? Explain why or why not.

Both prosecutors and defense attorneys try to discredit witnesses who testify for the other side in a criminal case. One way attorneys try to discredit trial witnesses is by confronting them with "prior inconsistent statements." For example, a witness may have told the police that he or she saw a robbery and that the robber wore a red shirt. Later at trial, the witness may say that the robber wore a purple shirt.

5. Is a "prior inconsistent statement" always the same thing as a lie? Explain why or why not.

6. The author Mark Twain wrote, "If you tell the truth you don't have to remember anything."
   • Explain what you think Twain meant.

   • Do you agree with Twain? Explain why or why not.

The Rodney King Beating -------------------------------

SOMETIME AFTER MIDNIGHT on Sunday, March 3, 1991, Rodney King was driving with two of his friends north of Los Angeles. King, who had had some problems with the law before, committed a minor traffic violation. Because he did not immediately stop for the police officers who witnessed the traffic violation, other officers, including officers in a helicopter, joined the brief pursuit. At least fifteen police officers were present when King stopped his car.

Across the street, several people who lived in an apartment complex were awakened by the police helicopter. They witnessed several officers beating King. One resident of the apartment complex, George Holliday, videotaped approximately seven minutes of the incident. The video showed two officers beating King with their batons and kicking him. The beating lasted almost two minutes. One officer fired an electrical stun gun at King, and another officer occasionally walked up to King while he was lying on the ground and kicked him.

Although the police officers realized that at least twenty apartment residents were watching, they made no effort to stop King's beating. Holliday's videotape was released to the news media and shown on television stations around the world. Shortly after the incident, a survey found that over 90 percent of Los Angeles residents polled believed that the police had used too much force in arresting King.

Four police officers were put on trial in a California state court for the King beating a year later. One of the key pieces of evidence at the trial was the Holliday video. The members of the jury, all residents of Southern California, undoubtedly had already seen the video several times before on television. On April 29, 1992, the jury acquitted all four of the police officers charged in King's beating. Los Angeles mayor Tom Bradley angrily declared, "Today, the jury told the world that what we all saw with our own eyes was not a crime."

Unfortunately, many people in Los Angeles reacted violently to the acquittal of the officers. In five days of rioting, fifty-four people were killed, many were injured, and millions of dollars of property was destroyed. Over seven thousand people were arrested.

A year later, the four police officers were again tried for beating King. The second trial took place in federal court. This time, two of the officers were convicted and sent to prison.

(continued)

The Rodney King Beating -------------------------

Record your answers below. Use another sheet of paper, if necessary.

Many observers of the Rodney King case say that the video of King's beating, which at first shocked viewers, was shown so many times that it desensitized people. These observers say that jurors themselves may have become desensitized by repeated viewings of the video.

1. What does it mean to become "desensitized"?

2. Do you believe that if a person sees a violent image or series of images repeatedly that the person can become desensitized to other violent images that he or she sees? Explain why or why not.

While the jurors watched the video of King's beating repeatedly during the trial, both the prosecutor and the defense attorneys tried to influence the jurors' opinions as to what they were actually observing. The prosecutor tried to get the jurors to believe that the video showed the police officers using excessive force against King. The police officers' lawyers tried to get the jurors to believe that the video showed that the officers were using an appropriate degree of force in that situation.

3. How can another person influence what someone thinks they are seeing? Explain your answer.

Rodney King is an African American. Many observers have pointed to the fact that the fifteen police officers who were at the scene of the King beating, including the four officers who were tried for beating King, were all white. None of the jurors in the first criminal trial was African American. This jury said that the police officers were not guilty of a crime.

4. Does a person's race affect the way he or she perceives the behavior of his or her own race? Explain your answer.

5. Does a person's race affect the way he or she perceives the behavior of another race? Explain your answer.

Cinema Therapy -

POPULAR MOVIES APPEAL to their audiences in a variety of ways. Many people enjoy the adrenaline "rush" of an action film. Some enjoy watching the "good guy" defeat the "bad guy" in movies. Many moviegoers enjoy comedies. Sometimes, the humor lies in laughing *with* a character; sometimes, the humor lies in laughing *at* a character. In addition, though it has been said, "everybody likes a happy ending," sad movies have proved to be popular with audiences.

Some therapists now use movies to help people deal with important and perhaps troubling issues in their lives. Movies tell stories, and these stories about how people deal with issues may help others to deal with issues in their lives. Even when an issue may be a particularly troubling one, a movie can be helpful without being heavy and bleak. Both serious movies and not-so-serious movies can help people deal with the things that are happening in their lives.

Record your answers below. Use another sheet of paper, if necessary.

1. Think about some of the movies that you have seen over the last few years. Then think about some of the following situations that a friend might be going through. For each situation, which movie would you recommend that your friend watch to help him or her? Explain your reason for each recommendation.

Issue	Recommended Movie	Reasons for Recommendation
Parents are splitting up		
Having trouble with schoolwork		
Having trouble with friends		
Wondering or concerned about life after high school		
Having trouble dating		
Loneliness		
Death of a loved one		

2. Have you ever seen a movie that helped you deal with issues in your own life?

   If so, name the movie and explain how it helped.

   If not, explain why movies have not been helpful to you.

The Written Word Versus the Oral Word - - - - - - - - - - - -

DIFFERENT PEOPLE have different learning styles. Some people are primarily auditory learners—they learn best by hearing. Other people are primarily kinesthetic learners—they learn best by doing. Some people are visual learners—they learn best by seeing.

Record your answers below. Use another sheet of paper, if necessary.

1. Which type of learner do you think you are? Explain why.

Television arose during the late 1940s. This means that you are among the third generation of people who grew up with television in their homes.

2. Do you think television has caused more people to become visual learners? Explain why or why not.

3. Do you think television has caused more people to become kinesthetic learners? Explain why or why not.

4. Studies have shown that people better remember a story about a news event if they read it in a newspaper or a magazine, rather than if they see a story about the event on television. List and describe two reasons why you think this occurs.

5. Suppose there is an upcoming political election. You have been asked by your teacher to find out information about one of the candidates in the election. Which of the following media would you prefer to use to learn about the candidate? (Rank each in order of preference from 1 to 3.) Explain your reasons for each ranking.

   • television

   • internet

   • news magazine

Video Games -

AMERICANS SPENT MORE than $10 billion on video games and equipment in 2002. The best-selling game was "Grand Theft Auto: Vice City." Americans' enjoyment of video games probably comes as no surprise to you. Chances are that you yourself are a regular player of video games, as most games are sold to teenagers.

Record your answers below. Use another sheet of paper, if necessary.

1. The United States Army actively recruits young men and women to enlist for military service. One of the tools that the Army uses to encourage teenagers to consider military service is a video game. The game, distributed free by the Army on CD and by Internet download, contains violence and blood. Of course, members of the United States Army face the possibility of engaging in violence and bloodshed in combat. Do you think that distributing a violent video game to try to recruit teenagers to join the Army is a good idea? Explain why or why not.

The amount of violence in video games has been a matter of controversy for a number of years. An organization called Children Now conducted a study that concluded in 2001[1]. Children Now found that

- most of the top-selling video games (89 percent) contained violent content, almost half of which was serious in nature.
- killing was almost always seen as justified in the games, and players were always rewarded for their acts of violence.
- the negative consequences of violence were rarely shown, with most victims appearing unaffected by the aggressive acts committed against them.
- more than three fourths of games rated "E" for "Everyone" (79 percent) contained violent content.
- male and female character roles and behaviors were frequently stereotyped, with males more likely to engage in physical aggression and females more likely to scream, wear revealing clothing, and be nurturing.

---

[1] www.childrennow.org/media/video-games/2001/fair-play-2001.pdf

(continued)

Video Games- -

2. Why do you think that violence is a characteristic of most video games? Explain your answer.

3. Not all of Children Now's findings about video games were negative. The organization acknowledged that video games can also be educational. Describe one way that video games can be used to teach a school subject to middle school or high school students.

4. "Educational technology" includes audiovisual equipment, computers, and other multimedia devices that help students learn. Over the past few years, many schools have spent increasing amounts of money on educational technology. Do you think this trend toward increased use of educational technology has helped you personally as a student? Explain your answer.

Different people have different learning styles. As discussed in Activity 7 in this unit, some people are primarily visual learners (they learn by seeing), some people are primarily kinesthetic learners (they learn by doing), and some people are primarily auditory learners (they learn by hearing).

5. Suppose that you have just received a new video game that you have never played before. The game comes with a ten-page manual of instructions about how to play the game. Which of the following best describes how you would learn the new game? Explain why.

   - I would play the game first and read the instruction manual only if I got confused.

   - I would ignore the instruction manual and learn the game by playing it.

   - I would first read the instruction manual completely before playing the game.

   - I would read a little bit of the instruction manual to get started and then would begin playing the game. I would only refer to the instruction manual again if I got confused.

(continued)

Video Games- -

6. Different people have different types of skills. What skills do players need to play most video games? List three, and explain each.

    •

    •

    •

7. Do most video games reward only those players who win? Or do most video games reward all players? Explain your answer.

8. Do you think people who play video games are able to make decisions for themselves as they play the game? Or do you think the decisions involving the playing of the game have already been made by the game's designers? Explain your answer.

9. Suppose you are a video game designer. Write a brief essay of three to five paragraphs to describe what your next new game would be about. In your essay, make sure you discuss each of the following issues.

    • In what location(s) would the game be set? Explain.

    • What choices would players be able to make about how they play the game? Explain.

    • Would the game be violent? Explain why or why not.

    • What would a player have to do to win the game? Explain.

    • What would you name this new game? Why?

The objectives of this unit are to help students

- understand the impact of color on human thought, attitudes, and activities
- enhance their writing skills
- generate creative responses to a variety of situations

MANY CHILDREN do not know how to read and write when they begin school. However, most children have learned color literacy before their formal education begins. Humans view color identification as an essential skill. This unit provides a series of exercises that attempt to engage the student in a more advanced exploration of the role of color in society. The goal is to use thinking about color to help students develop their creativity, empathy, rhetorical skills, and analytical ability.

In this Unit. . .

Color Blindness has students evaluate the impact of color blindness. Students also explore the role of color in daily activities.

Naming Colors, Describing Colors encourages students to rely on their creativity and language skills in naming and describing a group of colors.

What Color Is Confusion? has students explore the use of colors to describe emotions and abstract concepts.

Describe Blue challenges students to generate a written description of the color blue for a blind person.

Which Is Your Favorite Color? provides students with data on color preferences in different countries and different regions of the United States. Students undertake the task of articulating why a particular color is their favorite. Students also use data to identify patterns in color preferences.

Passive Pink offers students the opportunity to explore the psychological aspects of color in different environments.

The Pink Artichokes and the Rainbow Warriors introduces students to several true situations in which athletic team colors played a role in larger controversies, and asks students to evaluate the nature of those controversies.

A New Kind of Coloring Book has students assess critiques of traditional children's coloring books. Students also describe how they would produce a drawing of an abstract concept and design a rubric for evaluating a young child's drawn depiction of an abstraction.

COLOR HAS MEANING. For example, we identify the United States with red, white, and blue, the colors of the American flag. In December, many American households are decorated with red and green, colors associated with Christmas. In other American households, the month of December is associated with blue and silver, the colors associated with Hanukkah. In still other American households during December we can find decorations of red, black, and green, the colors of Kwanza.

> **"Color has meaning."**

Now imagine that you have just entered a convenience store or a grocery store. Quick— which brand of soda comes in a blue can? Which brand comes in a red can? If a soda is lemon-lime flavored, what color can does it come in? If you want a can of diet soda, which color should you look for? Colors are so effective for helping people identify particular products that some companies have obtained trademark protection for the exclusive use of certain colors for their product. Quick—what color is fiberglass? Are you sure?

In this unit, we will investigate the way people use color. We will look at the way color affects people. We will also explore the relationship between color and language.

Color Blindness-------------------------------------

THE FORMAL TERM for color blindness is "achromatopsia." Males are more likely to suffer from color blindness. Approximately eight percent of American males are color-blind. Less than one half of one percent of American females are color-blind. Red-green color blindness is by far the most common type of color blindness. A few people suffer from blue-yellow color blindness. Very few people (perhaps one in fifty thousand) are completely color-blind. Color blindness is genetic (passed down from one's parents). There is currently no known medical cure for color blindness. However, certain types of colored contact lenses can help some people.

Record your answers below. Use another sheet of paper, if necessary.

1. Blind people are able to develop ways of compensating for their blindness. Color-blind people also develop ways to compensate. For example, a traffic light features red and green lights. How would a color-blind person know which light is which?

2. Should people who are red-green color-blind legally be allowed to drive? Explain why or why not.

One of the things that bothers color-blind people is watching the weather on television. The weather map relies on color to provide viewers with information. Color-blind people often have difficulty interpreting the weather map. There are other problems for color-blind people while watching television.

3. Watch television with the sound turned down for a few minutes. Flip among different channels. List and describe three problems (other than reading the weather map) that you think a color-blind person would have.

   •

   •

   •

   Now turn the sound back up. Can color-blind people use sounds to help them compensate for color blindness? Explain why or why not.

(continued)

Activity 1 *(continued)*

Color Blindness- -

4. Color blindness is not associated with general blindness. In other words, a color-blind person may still enjoy 20/20 vision. However, color blindness may be a problem for certain types of occupations. Explain why it would be difficult for a color-blind person to work as a professional chef.

5. List three other occupations for which you think a color-blind person may not be qualified. Explain each.

    •

    •

    •

6. Explain why a color-blind person might have difficulty on a sunny day at the beach.

7. What three activities that you do nearly every day would be different if you were color blind (which you may be, especially if you are a male)? Explain each.

    •

    •

    •

Naming Colors, Describing Colors -

THERE ARE HUNDREDS of different names for colors of paint. There are also hundreds of different names for nail-polish colors and many different names for the colors of cars. Of course, a good color needs a good name to help sell that color. If you want to sell a particular shade of green paint, naming it "Puke" would probably hurt sales of that shade, no matter how pretty it is. (Although some of us have friends who would like a color called "Puke.") If you named that color "Spring Willow," some people may be encouraged to buy it because of its name.

Some manufacturers use color consultants to name the colors of their products. For example, one consultant names over six thousand colors each year for its clients.[1] There is even a not-for-profit association of "color professionals," the Color Marketing Group.

Record your answers below. Use another sheet of paper, if necessary.

1. Find an old magazine with lots of color photographs in it. Look through the photographs to find four colors that you think are interesting. Cut out a small piece of each of those four colors and tape or glue them to the page below. For each, come up with a descriptive name and explain why you believe it describes that color well.

Color sample	Your name for that color	Explanation for name choice
☐		
☐		
☐		
☐		

---

[1] Source: Color Services & Associates, Inc.: geocities.com/patscolor/services.htm

(continued)

Naming Colors, Describing Colors -

2. For each of the words or phrases below, provide a sample of what you think that color looks like. You can use crayon, markers, or glued pieces of color photographs.

Object/Event/Idea	Your color choice	Explanation for color choice
Broken		
Sauce		
Energy		
September		

What Color Is Confusion? — — — — — — — — — — — — — — — — — — —

YOU HAVE PROBABLY HEARD a jealous person described as being "green with envy." When a person is sad, he or she is described as feeling blue. Cowards are called yellow. Consider, then, each of the following.

Record your answers below. Use another sheet of paper, if necessary.

1. What feeling would you use the color orange to express? Explain why.

2. What feeling would you use the color purple to express? Explain why.

3. What feeling would you use the color red to express? Explain why.

4. What color is "confusion"? Explain why.

5. What color is "lazy"? Explain why.

6. What color is "love"? Explain why.

7. What color is "ugly"? Explain why.

Describe Blue —

IN UNIT 1, you explored the challenges of describing a large commercial jet to a blind person. Here, the task is to describe a color to a blind person.

Record your answers below. Use another sheet of paper, if necessary.

1. Of all the different colors, which one do you think would be the most difficult to describe to a blind person? Why?

2. Which color do you think would be the easiest to describe to a blind person? Why?

3. Suppose you have a blind friend. Your friend has excellent senses of smell, hearing, touch, and taste. He or she asks you to describe the color blue. Provide a description that helps your friend to understand what blue looks like. (*Hint:* Think about your friend's use of senses other than sight when developing your description of each color.) In three paragraphs with at least three sentences each, describe the color blue for your friend. Proofread by reading your description out loud, as you would for your blind friend.

Which Is Your Favorite Color? -

IF YOUR FAVORITE COLOR is blue, you are among the 44 percent of Americans who say that blue is their favorite color. Americans list blue, green, red, and black as their four top favorite colors. If your favorite color is yellow, you are among only 2 percent of Americans who say that is their favorite. White is also listed by 2 percent of Americans as their favorite.

In the African nation of Kenya, blue is also listed as the favorite color, but only by 29 percent of those polled. Purple is the favorite of 10 percent of Kenyans. Purple receives only 4 percent of the votes for favorite color among Americans. White is named by 9 percent of Kenyans. In Italy, blue finishes in first place again (27 percent). Yellow finishes in a strong fourth place among Italians, with 9 percent of the votes—more than four times as popular as it is among Americans. Black, named by 4 percent of Americans as their favorite color, receives three times as many votes in Portugal. Thirteen percent of the Portuguese cite black as their favorite color.[1]

It is relatively simple for a person to identify his or her favorite color. However, one person may like different colors depending on the item in question. For example, one's favorite color for clothes may be different from his or her favorite color for a car. People may also have different preferences for colors depending on the mood they are in. They may like bright colors when they are in a good mood, and pale or dull colors when not in a good mood.

Record your answers below. Use another sheet of paper, if necessary.

1. Explaining why a certain color is one's favorite can be challenging. It can be as hard as describing what water tastes like. You, however, must now list your favorite color and explain why it is your favorite color.

Henry Ford, the founder of the car company that bears his name, once said of his famous Model T that it came in one's choice of colors as long as that color was black. Alfred Sloan, the head of General Motors, offered cars in a choice of colors. This was because Sloan realized that a car is more than just a method of transportation. For many motorists, the color of their car is an extension of their personality.

2. Who do you think is more likely to drive a red car—a high school student or a high school teacher? Explain your answer.

_____

[1] Source: diacenter.org/km/surveyresults.html

(continued)

Which Is Your Favorite Color? -

3. "Arrest me red" is a term often used to describe the color of a car. Why do you think police officers may be more likely to give a speeding ticket to the driver of a red car than to drivers of cars of other colors?

One of the colors that American adults say they like the least is orange. However, studies have shown that American teenagers are much more attracted to orange than adults are.

4. Explain why you think there is a difference in acceptance of orange among these different age groups.

Besides personality characteristics, regional characteristics may affect a person's choice of colors. Students at twenty-six different elementary, middle, and high schools across the United States conducted a survey of car colors between 1998 and 2002.[2]

The survey found that cars in Arizona and New Mexico were rarely black. Forty-four percent of the cars in those two states were white, the highest percentage of white cars tallied in the country.

5. Why do you think black cars are so unpopular in Arizona and New Mexico, while white cars are very popular?

6. Consider the results in Arizona and New Mexico. What would you predict about the popularity of black cars in Florida? Why?

7. The lowest percentage of white cars was discovered to be in the northeastern United States, which includes states such as Massachusetts and Michigan. Why do you think white cars are relatively unpopular in that region?

---

[2] Source: www2.milwaukee.k12.wi.us/douglas/Map.HTML

Passive Pink -

A NUMBER OF YEARS AGO, the University of Iowa and Colorado State University applied pink paint on the walls of the visiting team's locker rooms at their football stadiums. This was done in the belief that pink makes players passive. The Western Athletic Conference (WAC) is a college sports league that includes the University of Hawaii and Boise State University. The WAC now has a rule that the visiting team's locker room cannot be painted a different color than the home team's locker room. The locker rooms can be any color a school wants to paint them, as long as they are the same color.[1]

Record your answers below. Use another sheet of paper, if necessary.

1. Why would colleges paint the visiting football team's locker room pink? Explain your answer.

In some prisons and jails, officials sometimes paint the walls a shade of pink known as Baker-Miller Pink. This shade of pink has been compared to the color of bubble gum.

2. Why do correctional facilities have pink walls? Explain your answer.

3. Now consider the opposite effect of passivity—aggression. What wall-paint color(s) do you believe would make people more aggressive? Explain why.

4. Who would want to use wall-paint colors that cause aggression? Explain why.

Imagine you have been asked to choose the colors to paint two rooms in someone's home—the bedroom and the dining room. Do not be concerned with style. Instead, focus on the activity that takes place in each room.

5. What color(s) would you use for the bedroom? Explain why.

6. What color(s) would you use for the dining room? Explain why.

---

[1] *Honolulu Star-Bulletin* 10/24/99

The Pink Artichokes and the Rainbow Warriors --------

IN THE EARLY 1970s, many students at Scottsdale Community College in Arizona were upset at the college administration's plans to emphasize sports. These students thought the administration was not emphasizing academics as much as it should. As a way of protesting, students held an election and voted for the artichoke as the college's mascot. They also voted for pink as the college's athletic color. Although the college has changed its athletic teams' colors, its teams are still known as the Artichokes.

The Scottsdale Community College Artichoke

Record your answers below. Use another sheet of paper, if necessary.

1. Why would voting for the color pink as a school's athletic color be seen as a protest against athletics?

2. What would be your reaction if your school adopted pink and white for its athletic colors? Explain.

The athletic teams at the University of Hawai'i had been known as the Rainbows since 1923. The teams also began using the name Rainbow Warriors in the 1960s. The university's sports teams had the colors of the rainbow on their uniform, and the football team had a rainbow logo on their helmets.

University of Hawai'i Rainbow Warriors

In 2000, the University of Hawai'i changed its athletic teams' nickname from Rainbow Warriors to Warriors. The teams' logo was also changed from a design that featured a rainbow to the letter *H* in green, white, and black. Some Hawaiians liked the name and design change. Many others were unhappy.

University of Hawai'i Warriors

The university changed the teams' name and logo for several reasons. One reason was the desire to sell more clothing and other items with the university's name on them. The university believed that the new look was more appealing to fans than the old look.

(continued)

The Pink Artichokes and the Rainbow Warriors ------

3. Do you think it is okay to change a school's traditional sports nickname and school colors if the change will help the school make more money? Explain your answer.

Hugh Yoshida, the university's athletic director, explained another reason for the change. "That [rainbow] logo really put a stigma on our program at times, in regards to its part of the gay community, their flags and so forth," Yoshida said. Several gay and lesbian organizations expressed their disappointment with Yoshida's remark.

4. Explain why you think Yoshida's comment angered some gay people.

A change of athletic nicknames can also be used to prevent people's feelings from being hurt. The Stanford University Indians became the Cardinal (the color, not the bird) in 1979. The St. John's University Redmen became the Red Storm in 1995.

5. Why do you think these two universities changed their athletic teams' nickname?

A New Kind of Coloring Book -

YOU PROBABLY USED coloring books as a child. These books typically contain black and white outlines of various characters, objects, or shapes. A child fills in the outlines using colored crayons, paint, and so forth.

Record your answers below. Use another sheet of paper, if necessary.

1. Some educators criticize coloring books. They say that coloring books do not help, and could hurt, the development of a child's creativity. Why do you think they say this?

2. Do you agree or disagree with this criticism of coloring books? Explain your answer.

3. If an adult says another adult "colors outside of the lines," what does that mean? Explain.

An alternative to a traditional coloring book is a book that encourages children to create their own drawings. For example, consider a coloring book that emphasizes ideas about America. Instead of providing the black and white outline of the United States flag, the coloring book could ask the child to draw the flag themselves. To help the child begin, the page of the coloring book could show a flagpole without a flag on the pole.

However, even this exercise may not encourage creativity as much as possible. After all, there already is a design for the United States flag. All we would be asking the child to do is reproduce it. Let us take the idea of a coloring book about America to the next step. Instead of providing a specific object for children to draw, let's use an idea or a feeling. For example, the directions in the coloring book could ask the child to draw a picture that represents "freedom." Obviously, there is not just one clearly defined object that represents freedom.

4. If a young child asked you what freedom looked like, what would you draw? Explain your answer.

(continued)

A New Kind of Coloring Book -

Let us look at another effort to draw an idea or a feeling rather than an object. Suppose you asked a young child to draw a picture that shows "happiness." Just as with the idea of "freedom," there is no single best way to depict "happiness" in a drawing. But presume that you are going to assign a grade to this drawing. The grade will be on a three point scale: needs improvement, average, and excellent.

Before grading an assignment, teachers often create a checklist or "rubric" for that assignment. This rubric explains how each grade is assigned. The purpose of the rubric is to help teachers grade fairly. It also helps the teacher provide constructive criticism. Some teachers will explain their rubric when giving an assignment so that the student knows what is expected of him or her. The challenge here is to provide enough information to help the child understand what is expected without providing so much information that creativity is discouraged.

5. Write a rubric for grading a drawing of "happiness" by describing the three-point grading system you will use.

   Assignment: Draw a picture that depicts "happiness."

   • Needs improvement (why is the drawing below average?)

   • Average (why is the drawing average, but not excellent?)

   • Excellent (why is the drawing better than average?)

The objectives of this unit are to help students

- understand that standards of human attractiveness are culturally and historically bound
- recognize how gender and racial stereotypes affect perception of oneself and of others
- identify the social factors that contribute to people's desire to alter or modify their bodies

ANY TEACHER of teenagers knows how much emphasis teenagers place on the appearance of themselves and of others. Social belonging, self-esteem, and the transition to adulthood emerge as powerful factors in teenagers' lives. Facial features, body types, and fashion receive intense scrutiny. This unit uses these common concerns as the basis of a series of activities in which students investigate various perspectives of how society regards the human body.

In this Unit. . .

Why Is Thin In? has students explore cultural and gender differences in the perception of ideal body weight. Students also are asked to identify some of the causes of eating disorders and to consider how best to address the needs of a friend who may be suffering from an eating disorder.

Tattoo You? has students investigate the reasons for the recent surge in popularity of tattoos.

The Good, the Bad, and the Victimized provides students with an opportunity to analyze how television programs present visual cues to identify goodness, evil, and victimization.

What Is Attractive in America? is an effort to have students assess stereotypical notions of human beauty and gender distinctions in appearance.

Plastic Surgery asks students to evaluate the reasons that people elect plastic surgery, and requires students to determine when it is appropriate to ask others to help pay for a person's surgery. Students also examine the criticism of pop singer Michael Jackson's efforts to change his appearance.

The Hairy President presents historical information about American presidents as the basis of students' investigation into the role facial appearance plays in politics.

"You're Not Leaving the House Looking Like That!" has students explore the relationship between fashion and social identification.

IN THE LATE 1800s, the United States was in the midst of the Industrial Revolution. Factories were built across the country. The lure of factory jobs drew many young men and women from rural farming communities to fast-growing cities. City life was different from country life in many ways. One of the things young people found different was dating. In small farming communities, young people grew up together and knew each other their entire lives. In the city, almost everybody was a stranger. People had to learn how to make intelligent decisions about other people based on much less information than they were used to having. While appearances were considered important, it was also known that looks could deceive.

> **"No one is born ugly. Nor is anyone born attractive."**

Today, we have access to cosmetics and dyes to change our appearances. Clothing can highlight some parts of a person's body and conceal other parts. Some of us will use plastic surgery to add to, remove, or rearrange body parts. People's efforts to modify their appearance are typically based on idealized concepts of beauty and body types. Because most of the United States' population has historically been of European heritage, the American cultural views of idealized beauty and body types have tended to be based on European ideals. However, with the number of Americans of Asian, African, and Latin American heritage increasing, there may be a change in how Americans view the human body.

Despite changes in how the body is viewed, a basic reality of American culture that seems to be unchanged is the social pressure placed on females to be more concerned about cosmetics and fashion than males are. While this may seem basic to humans, remember that the situation is reversed among birds. Male birds, with their brightly colored feathers and impressive plumage, are more spectacular than their relatively drab female counterparts. But one doubts that a male bird with dull feathers suffers from low self-esteem and a lack of dates. Humans are not as kind.

No one is born ugly. Nor is anyone born attractive. How we define these terms is based on what we are taught—not formally, but informally. Today, the media play a large role in determining what our view of attractiveness is. The study of visual culture is the study of how we perceive what we see. In this unit, we will look at how we perceive the human body.

Why Is Thin In? -------------------------------

MANY AMERICAN DOCTORS consider a person overweight if he or she is 25–35 pounds above the maximum desirable weight for a certain height. You probably already know that there are several factors that make it more likely for some groups of people to be overweight than other groups of people. You probably also know that some people have physical or medical conditions that make it almost impossible for them to maintain the desirable weight for their height.

Studies have found that when shown pictures or drawings of a thin person and an overweight person, American children are more likely to identify the thin person as the healthier of the two. That might not surprise you. But when children are asked to guess which of the two people shown is the hardest worker, they are also more likely to choose the thin person. The same result occurs when children are asked to guess which of the two people shown is the smartest. This is a form of prejudice. *Prejudice* is a word that is often incorrectly used. Its true meaning is to prejudge a person or situation based on insufficient information about that particular person or situation.

Record your answers below. Use another sheet of paper, if necessary.

1. Why do you think American children often demonstrate prejudice about overweight people? Explain your answer.

Different cultures have different attitudes about the appropriate weight for a person. Some cultures value large body types that would be considered overweight in today's United States. Among the Matsigenka people, a tribe in the South American nation of Peru, men often identify the heaviest women as the healthiest and most attractive. This is also true of the men of the Hazda people in Tanzania, an African nation.

2. Why do you think that some cultures prefer heavier women and others prefer thinner women? Explain your answer.

3. Do you think most American males are
   • more concerned about their weight than females,
   • equally concerned about their weight,
   • or less concerned about their weight than females?

Explain your answer.

(continued)

Why Is Thin In? -

4. Think of famous entertainers—musicians and movie stars—who are overweight by American standards. Which gender has more overweight entertainers—men or women? Who has an easier chance of becoming a well-known entertainer—an overweight male or an overweight female? Explain why you think this is the case.

5. Most models in American fashion magazines and advertisements are thin, certainly thinner than the average person in real life. Some critics argue that these images of unusually thin people make members of the public unhappy with their own bodies. Do you agree? Explain why or why not.

You probably know that millions of American females, and many males, suffer from eating disorders. A common disorder is anorexia nervosa, a psychological condition in which people—in order to make themselves abnormally thin—refuse to eat as much food as they should. Another common disorder is bulimia nervosa, in which a person binges on large amounts of food, then tries to purge the body by vomiting or abusing laxatives to force defecation. Some people who suffer from bulimia do not purge themselves, but follow uncontrolled overeating with excessive exercise or fasting.

6. Studies have shown that the average (mean) age for the onset of anorexia in females is seventeen. Explain what you think is going on in the lives of teenage females who suffer from anorexia or bulimia.

7. The best way to help a friend who may be suffering from anorexia or bulimia is to encourage them to seek professional counseling. What would you say to a friend whom you suspected of suffering from anorexia or bulimia? Explain your answer.

Tattoo You? -

TATTOOS ON HUMAN SKIN have been around for many centuries. However, in the United States and other countries, tattoos have experienced a new surge in popularity. The popularity of tattoos is strongest among teenagers and young adults.

Record your answers below. Use another sheet of paper, if necessary.

1. Imagine that our friend Chilly has been frozen in a block of ice for twenty years. Chilly has recently thawed out and is surprised to see how many more people are getting tattoos today than they were twenty years ago. He asks you why. What would you tell Chilly?

2. People in their forties, fifties, and sixties are also getting tattoos today. Ask older adults why they think some people their age get tattoos, and write down what those older adults tell you.

   • Do you think older people get tattoos for reasons different from teenagers' reasons, or for the same reasons? Explain your answer.

3. According to the American Society of Dermatology (an organization of doctors who specialize in skin problems) more than 50 percent of those who have a tattoo in the United States will later want it removed. That figure rises to almost 70 percent for married people. Why do you think more married people want tattoos removed than single people? Explain your answer.

4. Tattoo parlors typically have many examples of tattoo designs displayed in their front windows and hanging on their walls. Some tattoo enthusiasts look down on these predesigned tattoos, calling them "flash." Why do you think some people who like tattoos do not like predesigned tattoos? Explain your answer.

(continued)

Tattoo You? -------------------------------------

5. A number of professional athletes have been asked to get corporate tattoos. These tattoos would feature the logo, or trademark, for a company. In exchange, the companies have offered to pay the athletes a significant amount of money. Suppose you are a famous athlete or some other type of famous celebrity. A large company offers you a million dollars to get a tattoo with their logo on it. Would you get the tattoo? Explain why or why not.

6. Find somebody who has a tattoo and ask why he or she got it. Write down what you learned here. Do you think their reason was a good one? Explain why or why not.

7. If you were going to get a tattoo, what would it look like? Draw it here:

9. Explain why you drew the design that you did.

10. Do you think that someday you might get a tattoo? Explain why or why not.

The Good, the Bad, and the Victimized -----------------

IN TELEVISION DRAMAS, especially police dramas, there is usually a conflict between good and evil. The most common way of displaying this is as a conflict between two or more characters (person against person, more formally called "local conflict"). One person represents good, and the other represents evil. Most television dramas are one hour long. However, after subtracting time used during that hour by commercials, the average television drama is really about forty-five minutes long. In those forty-five minutes, the characters must be introduced, their conflict must be introduced, and their conflict must be resolved.

The good person (or persons) is usually a regular character on the program, so if the viewer is familiar with the program, he or she may already know that character is a good person. This good person will be placed in conflict with one or more bad people. These bad people are rarely regular characters on the program, so the fact that he or she is bad must quickly be established. Certainly, what the character does or says helps the viewer understand that the character is a bad person.

Television is a highly visual medium. After all, we do not say we "listen" to television, we say we "watch" it. Because of the visual nature of television, the bad character will usually "look the part." In those cases where part of the element of surprise in a television program is that a character we think is good turns out really to be bad, his or her evilness is typically concealed by their "good" appearance.

Record your answers below. Use another sheet of paper, if necessary.

1. In the space below, draw a "good" person.

(continued)

The Good, the Bad, and the Victimized – – – – – – – – – – – – –

2. In the space below, draw a "bad" person.

3. Is your good person male or female? Explain why you chose that gender.

   • What kind of clothes does he or she wear? Why?

   • What color is his or her skin? Why?

   • How old is your good person? Why?

4. Is your bad person male or female? Explain why you chose that gender.

   • What kind of clothes does he or she wear? Why?

   • What color is his or her skin? Why?

   • How old is your bad person? Why?

(continued)

The Good, the Bad, and the Victimized - - - - - - - - - - - - - -

5. Are most characters that are good people on television programs male or female? Why do you think the people who create television programs often choose that gender to represent goodness?

6. Are most characters that are bad people on television programs male or female? Why do you think the people who create television programs often choose that gender to represent evil?

7. What color of skin do most characters that are good people on television programs have? Why do you think the people who create television programs often choose that skin color to represent goodness?

8. In the space below, draw a "victim."

(continued)

The Good, the Bad, and the Victimized -------------

9. Is your victim male or female? Explain why you chose that gender.

   • What kind of clothes does he or she wear? Why?

   • What color is his or her skin? Why?

   • How old is your victim? Why?

10. What color skin do most characters that are victims on television programs have? Why do you think the people who create television programs often choose that skin color for victims?

11. Are most characters that are victims on television programs male or female? Why do you think the people who create television programs often choose that gender for victims?

What Is Attractive in America? -

THE CONCEPT OF attractiveness is not the same in every culture. Different cultures have different ideas about what an attractive male or an attractive female looks like. As mentioned in Activity 1 in this unit, different cultures have different ideas about the ideal weight for a female.

Suppose that Marvin and Martina Martian have recently arrived on Earth from Mars. The concept of attractiveness is different on Mars. Marvin, for example, is admired by Martian females because he has three eyes; most Martian males have four, but three is considered more desirable. Martina is admired by many Martian males because her skin is a particularly lovely shade of green, with just the right purple highlights. Marvin and Martina have never been to Earth before. When they return, they know that they will be asked the following questions by their fellow Martians. Help them answer the questions.

Record your answers below. Use another sheet of paper, if necessary.

1. Which color hair is considered the most attractive for American females? What evidence could you find in stores to prove this?

2. What color eyes are considered the most attractive for Americans? What evidence would you use to prove this?

3. Is it more desirable for American males to be taller than average or shorter than average? What evidence would you use to prove this?

4. Is it more desirable for American females to be taller than average or shorter than average? What evidence would you use to prove this?

5. Is it considered most desirable for a female to be taller than her male partner or shorter? Why?

(continued)

What Is Attractive in America? -

6. Who is supposed to have more body hair—males or females? What evidence would you use to prove this?

7. In consideration of your answers to number 6, can the more hairy of the two genders have too much hair? Explain your answer.

8. Is it considered more desirable among Americans to have curly hair or straight hair? Can hair be too curly? Can hair be too straight? Explain why or why not.

9. Can a female be attractive without wearing makeup?

10. Why do many females in American society wear makeup?

11. Why do most men in American society not wear makeup?

12. Are there social situations in which a female should wear makeup? Explain why or why not.

Plastic Surgery ---

MANY PEOPLE are uncomfortable or unhappy with their appearance. Sometimes, a person's discomfort or unhappiness with their appearance is created by idealized images of men and women in fashion magazines and other media. Many photographs of beautiful women and handsome men in magazines are the result of hours of work by teams of make-up artists, special photography techniques, and extensive use of editing devices to change a person's appearance. Recent advances in digital photography and digital photo editing make this increasingly common.

Sometimes, a person's discomfort or unhappiness with their appearance may be easily understood by others. For example, there are situations when a person is born without a fully developed ear, or has suffered a disfiguring scar on an area of the body where it can be easily seen. Other people have had their bodies disfigured by illness or disease.

Many of us have health insurance. When we are insured, we are part of an insurance pool. The idea here is that most people who are insured by a single company will not be seriously ill during any given period of time. In turn, we help pay for the medical costs of those few members who do need expensive medical care during that period. If there is an outbreak of illness or disease among people insured by a particular insurance company, health care costs go up. These costs are passed along to all members through increased insurance payments.

Some medical procedures are considered necessary. These procedures are needed in order to save a person's life or to help reduce significant pain. Necessary procedures include treatment of cancer and other severe illnesses. Some medical procedures are considered elective. Elective procedures are for physical conditions that are not considered serious or life-threatening. Many plastic-surgery procedures are considered elective procedures.

Record your answers below. Use another sheet of paper, if necessary.

The American Medical Association and the American Society of Plastic Surgeons make the following distinctions between reconstructive surgery and cosmetic surgery:

> Reconstructive surgery is performed on abnormal structures of the body, caused by congenital [birth] defects, developmental abnormalities, trauma [injury], infection, tumors or disease. It is generally performed to improve function, but may also be done to approximate a normal appearance.

> Cosmetic surgery is performed to reshape normal structures of the body in order to improve the patient's appearance and self-esteem.

(continued)

Plastic Surgery -

1. If people want to use their own money to have plastic surgery, should they be able to have that surgery? Answer this question for each of the following procedures. For each, explain why or why not.

   • Abdominoplasty—a "tummy tuck"

   • Blepharoplasty—propping up droopy eyelids; for some people this is a purely cosmetic procedure, while for others this procedure may help their vision.

   • Mammoplasty:

      a. Breast augmentation—making a female's breasts larger

      b. Breast reconstruction—usually, for women who have had one or both breasts removed because of breast cancer

      c. Breast reduction—a procedure done when the patient believes that her breasts are too large; there may be social problems (being stared at) or physical problems (a bad back)

   • Otoplasty—"pinning back" ears that stick out from the head abnormally

   • Rhinoplasty—reducing the size, or otherwise changing the shape, of one's nose; for some people rhinoplasty improves breathing.

2. For this question, presume that a patient is poor or otherwise unable to pay for plastic surgery. In these situations, they want their health-care insurer to help them pay. This of course means that other members of the insurance company will be required to help pay for those procedures. If the patient is uninsured, he or she is hoping that the government will use taxpayers' money to pay for the surgery. Should an insurance company or the government help pay for the following procedures? For each, explain why or why not.

   • Abdominoplasty

   • Blepharoplasty

   • Mammoplasty:

      a. Breast augmentation

      b. Breast reconstruction

      c. Breast reduction

   • Otoplasty

   • Rhinoplasty

(continued)

Plastic Surgery -------------------------------

Some plastic surgeons have provided treatment for a reduced price or at no charge to patients who have some particularly disfiguring body features or scars. For example, some women who have had their noses disfigured as the result of domestic abuse have benefited from the generosity of plastic surgeons. Plastic surgery corrects the victims' facial appearance and removes a physical reminder of the abuse they have received. Some children who are born with facial features that cause them to be stared at and teased have also been helped by plastic surgeons' charity work. However, a plastic surgeon can rarely afford to donate his or her services to everybody who asks for them.

3. Should insurance companies (or in the case of uninsured people, the taxpaying public) help pay for plastic surgery for abused women? Explain why or why not.

4. Should insurance companies (or in the case of uninsured people, the taxpaying public) help pay for plastic surgery for children born with disfiguring facial features? Explain why or why not.

You are probably familiar with some of the criticism of the singer Michael Jackson's numerous surgeries by plastic surgeons. Some people, both African American and otherwise, have criticized Jackson, claiming that he has tried to replace his African-American facial features with European-American facial features.

5. Why do you think that some African-American people are unhappy about Jackson's decision to undergo plastic surgery? Explain your answer.

6. Why do you think that some people who are not African-American are unhappy about Jackson's decision to undergo plastic surgery? Explain your answer.

7. Do you believe that a person who has facial features that are not considered European-American should be able to pay to have plastic surgery to make them look European-American? Explain why or why not.

The Hairy President ----------------------------------

By 2004, forty-three men had served as president of the United States. Nine of them had a beard or a mustache. The first bearded president was Abraham Lincoln, who was president from 1861 to 1865. The last was William Howard Taft, who served from 1909 to 1913. During the period from Lincoln's presidency through Taft's, only two presidents lacked a beard or a mustache—Andrew Johnson (1861–1865) and William McKinley (1897–1901).

Record your answers below. Use another sheet of paper, if necessary.

Rutherford B. Hayes, United States President, 1877–1881

1. The last major political candidate for the U.S. presidency with a mustache was Thomas Dewey. Dewey ran unsuccessfully as the Republican Party's candidate in 1944 and 1948. During this period, two of the United States' biggest political enemies were Adolph Hitler of Germany and Joseph Stalin of the Soviet Union. Both Hitler and Stalin had mustaches. Do you think that Dewey's mustache contributed to his defeat in the 1944 and 1948 elections? Explain why or why not.

More recent political enemies of the United States have included Osama Bin Laden and Saddam Hussein. Bin Laden has a beard; Hussein has a mustache. When captured in December 2003, Hussein had a full beard.

2. Do you think an American with a beard or a mustache today should shave his facial hair if he is considering running for political office? Explain why or why not.

(continued)

The Hairy President ----------------------------------

Balding is caused by genetics—people inherit the tendency to lose their hair from one or both of their parents. Many men (and some women) lose hair as they age. Since U.S. presidents tend to be older than the average person (after often lengthy careers in business or other areas of government), many presidents have had some degree of balding. None, however, has been completely bald.

3. Do you think a completely bald person could be elected president of the United States today? Explain why or why not.

Television has had an impact on politics. The first televised debate between two candidates for president was broadcast live on September 26, 1960, the first of four presidential debates broadcast that fall. John F. Kennedy, a U.S. Senator from Massachusetts, was the Democratic candidate for president that year. Richard M. Nixon, the vice president of the nation, was the Republican candidate. Most observers agreed that Kennedy was more telegenic (looked better on television) than Nixon. Nixon had recently been hospitalized and appeared pale and tired. He perspired heavily and wore clothes that did not fit well because he had lost weight while in the hospital. Nixon also had thinning hair with a distinct widow's peak (a V-shaped area of hair in the middle of his forehead). Kennedy, on the other hand, had a flattering suntan and a thick head of hair. Since television is a visual medium, these details, generally ignored before in American politics, now were seen as important in winning elections. The presidential election in November 1960 gave such a narrow victory to Kennedy that many people believe that the televised debates were the difference in the presidential campaigns.

Surveys of people who listened to the first Kennedy-Nixon debate on the radio found that these listeners tended to believe that Nixon had won. Surveys of those who watched the debate on television found that viewers tended to believe that Kennedy had won.

4. What do you think is a good explanation for the different results of these surveys?

Political candidates know that it is important to appear attractive to the voting public. *Attractive* here does not necessarily mean sexually attractive. (Very few voters choose political candidates the same way they choose boyfriends and girlfriends!) However, appearance remains an important concern for most candidates.

5. How important should the appearance of a politician be? Why?

"You're Not Leaving the House Looking Like That!" -----

UNTIL ABOUT TWENTY years ago, a formally dressed woman in the United States was required to wear a dress. This custom has been relaxed somewhat. Until about forty years ago, a formally dressed man may have worn a hat. This custom has virtually disappeared, and stores that specialize in formal men's hats have nearly vanished from the American landscape. However, formally dressed men are still expected to wear neckties today. If you asked them why, most men would probably not be able to provide any reason other than "It is what I am supposed to do."

Fashion changes regularly. There are many reasons why fashion changes. Some reasons are related to changes in textiles. The invention of synthetic fibers proved to be a significant cause of change in popular fashions. The availability of nylon, rayon, and polyester, used by themselves or blended with natural fibers, changed the way many Americans dressed. For example, women's hosiery evolved from expensive silk stockings typically available only at fine department stores to inexpensive nylon pantyhose sold at grocery stores and convenience stores.

Another reason for changing fashions is changing social circumstances. Certainly, the changing attitudes about the importance of women in society caused by the women's liberation movement of the 1960s also influenced the popularization of pants and slacks for women at that time. Similarly, the civil rights movement encouraged African Americans, Latinos, and other minority groups to celebrate their cultures through the display of ethnic clothing.

Record your answers below. Use another sheet of paper, if necessary.

Formal fashions among older adults change much more gradually than the informal fashions of teenagers and young adults. This is due in part to the fact that formal attire is often expensive and represents a substantial investment. This is also because teenagers are much more interested in trends and are constantly seeking the latest fashions.

1. Where do the teenagers at your school or in your neighborhood get information about what fashions are in style? Explain your answer.

2. Are there some teenagers at your school or in your neighborhood who are quicker to adopt new fashions than most of the other teenagers? Explain your answer.

   • If so, are these teenagers trendsetters for others? Explain why or why not.

(continued)

"You're Not Leaving the House Looking Like That!" - - -

3. How many different styles of clothing are there among teenaged males at your school or in your neighborhood? List and describe each of them.

   • If you are a male, which group would you say you mostly belong in? Explain why.

4. How many different styles of clothing are there among teenaged females at your school or in your neighborhood? List and describe each of them.

   • If you are a female, which group would you say you mostly belong in? Explain why.

5. How important is it to you that you wear the current fashions? Explain your answer.

6. Would you guess that people your age in other parts of the United States dress the same way people in your neighborhood do? Explain why or why not.

7. Do you think most American teenagers, no matter where they live, use the same sources of information for deciding what fashions to wear? Explain why or why not.

8. Many people who study fashion point out that clothing styles popular with teenagers usually make their first appearance in inner cities. These styles are first adopted by African Americans, Latinos, and others, and the styles later spread among European-American and other teenagers in the suburbs. Explain why you think this happens.

9. Has an older adult ever told you, "You're not leaving the house looking like that"? If so, what was your reaction? Explain your answer.

The objectives of this unit are to help students

- recognize the social and political power that reading literacy confers
- understand that language in oral and written form is alive and ever changing
- appreciate how different languages and cultures interact with each other

READING AND WRITING are perhaps the most important things that a person learns in school. Indeed, the most basic definition of an educated person is one who can read and write. This unit discusses the written word in several historical and cultural contexts. Two activities examine the shared roots of the world's languages and writing systems. The significance of the appearance of the written word on a page is also examined. This unit strives to help students realize that language and writing, although bound by certain conventions, can also be manipulated and changed.

In this Unit. . .

Alphabets provides information about the world's different alphabet systems. Students use this information to answer questions about possible adaptations and modifications of the English alphabet over time.

Two Countries Divided by a Common Language is an Internet exercise in which students discover the different terms and phrases used by American English and British English for common items.

Borrowed Words and False Cognates has students explore the transmission of words among different languages, as well as examine the problem of false cognates.

Cambodians and Khmer asks students to consider the political consequences of literacy. Students also scrutinize the impact global media have on some lesser-used languages.

Literacy and Voting helps students examine the relationship between literacy and civic engagement, both in the United States and in other nations.

Which Font Do You Want? introduces students to the craft of typography and has students use their creativity to select appropriate typefaces for a variety of applications.

ANCIENT EGYPTIANS used a set of symbols called hieroglyphics to record information. Later, European explorers in Egypt discovered many examples of hieroglyphics carved in stone. However, the ability to understand what the hieroglyphics meant was lost sometime around 300 C.E. In 1799, a group of French soldiers discovered a slab of granite in Rascha (also known as Rosetta) a town near the Nile River in Egypt. This slab, which has become known as the Rosetta Stone, had carvings in two languages (Egyptian and Greek) and three scripts (hieroglyphics and another Egyptian script, as well as Greek). A French **linguist,** Jean François Champollion, stud-ied the Rosetta Stone for fourteen years. In 1822, he published his findings.

> **"Thanks to Champollion's work, we are now able to interpret a written language that had been unknown for nearly 1,500 years."**

Because Champollion could read Greek as well as some other languages, he was able to translate the ancient hieroglyphics. We now know that ancient Egyptians carved the stone in 196 B.C.E. to describe some of the rules made by the Egyptian pharaoh (ruler) Ptolemy the Fifth. Thanks to Champollion's work, we are now able to interpret a written language that had been unknown for nearly 1,500 years. *Rosetta Stone* has become part of our language today as a term describing any decrypting (decoding) device.

Today, a group of linguists are working on the Rosetta Project. The project is devoted to creating and recording written translations of one thousand existing languages. The Rosetta Project is designed to serve, if necessary, as an advanced Rosetta Stone, should some or all of those languages be lost sometime in the future. As we will see in this unit, languages and alphabets change over time, and many have become extinct. In the process, the meaning of the word *literacy* is also changing.

Alphabets -

YOU MAY ALREADY KNOW that the word *alphabet* comes from the first two letters in the Greek alphabet, alpha and beta. But there may be some things about alphabets that you do not know. Most of the world's languages use alphabets that can be grouped into several main categories, which include Latin or Roman (used in much of Europe and the western Hemisphere), Semitic (used in the Middle East), Sino-Tibetan (used in eastern Asia), and Indian-Dravidian (used in South and Southeast Asia).

Some facts about languages that use Latin alphabets:

- The English and American alphabets both use Latin letters and Arabic numbers. There are twenty-six letters in our alphabet.

- The Czech alphabet also uses Latin letters, but has thirty-eight of them.

- The Hawaiian alphabet has been Latinized into thirteen letters, including a letter that we refer to in English as the apostrophe. Thus, the preferred spelling of the fiftieth state is "Hawai'i."

- Tagalog, one of the languages used in the Philippines, has twenty Latin letters.

Non-Latin alphabets:

- The Greek alphabet of twenty-four letters is over 2,700 years old.

- Russia and some neighboring countries use a Cyrillic alphabet with thirty-three letters. Cyrillic letters are based on both the Latin and the Greek alphabet.

- Chinese, as you may know, has tens of thousands of characters. Characters called *pictographs* denote things (such as "horse"). *Ideographs* denote ideas or concepts (such as "strength"). To be considered literate by modern Chinese standards, a person needs to know about five thousand characters.

- Semitic languages, which include Arabic and Hebrew, are used throughout the Middle East.

- Indian-Dravidic languages are used in countries in South and Southeast Asia. These include Hindi, one of the many official languages of India.

Oral languages with no native alphabet:

- The Hmong language, used by some people in Southeast Asia, is only one example of an oral language with no alphabet of its own. Only recently have non-Hmong speakers attempted to transliterate Hmong into their own alphabets.

(continued)

Alphabets -

Colonialism had a tremendous impact on the use of languages and alphabets. For example, the English language and its alphabet spread as Great Britain colonized North America, some of the Caribbean islands, Hawai'i, South Africa, and India. The Spanish brought their language and alphabet to South America and the Philippines. The French took their language to parts of Africa, the Caribbean, and Southeast Asia. In an unusual move, the French decided to provide their own alphabet to the existing language of the Vietnamese. Prior to the French occupation of Vietnam, the Vietnamese language had used an alphabet similar to Chinese. Today, the Vietnamese language uses thirty-seven Latin characters.

After this brief introduction to the alphabets of different cultures, consider the following questions.

Record your answers below. Use another sheet of paper, if necessary.

1. The English alphabet, with Latin characters (letters), is used by most Americans. Our alphabet has twenty-six letters. Are all of those letters necessary? Explain why or why not.

2. Regardless of how you answered question 1, presume that you have been given the task of eliminating three letters in the English alphabet.
   • Which three would you get rid of?

   • Explain your reasons for eliminating each letter.

Several languages, including Spanish and Vietnamese, use diacritics, also called **diacritical marks.** These marks are often placed over vowels to help the readers and speakers correctly read and pronounce a letter. For example, a long *a* may be written "ā." Similarly, a diacritical mark may be used to help the reader or speaker place emphasis on the correct syllable in a word, such as in the word "olé." Some diacritical marks occur with consonants, such as in the French feminine name Françoise. The hook below the *c* is called a *cedilla.* Here, the cedilla tells us that the letter is pronounced as a soft *c,* with an *s* sound rather than a hard *k* sound.

(continued)

Alphabets --

3. One example of an English word that uses a diacritical mark is "naïve." Find at least one other commonly used word in English that uses a diacritical mark and write it here.

4. Some languages that use the Latin alphabet have more letters than English because they count some letters that include diacritical marks as separate letters. Do you think English would be easier to read and pronounce if we included more diacritical marks in our language? Explain why or why not.

Languages and alphabets can change over time. Letters can be added to the alphabet, and letters can be lost. For example, when the United States was founded in 1776, it was then a common practice to use the symbol *ſ* instead of the letter *s* in some cases. This practice is no longer common today.

You are probably familiar with *emoticons*. These use typed letters to convey emotions, such as " :) ."

5. Explain how an emoticon is similar to a Chinese ideogram, described on page 97.

6. Do you think that emoticons may eventually be added to the English alphabet? Explain why or why not.

Two Countries Divided by a Common Language ----------

THE TITLE OF THIS activity comes from a quotation by the playwright George Bernard Shaw (1856–1950). Shaw's full quotation is, "England and America are two countries divided by a common language." The United States began as a group of British colonies of which most citizens were English speakers. However, the English language has changed since the United States achieved independence from Britain in 1776. New words, or new uses of existing words, have arisen in each country since that time.

Record your answers below. Use another sheet of paper, if necessary.

1. Using an Internet search engine, such as Google (google.com) or Excite (excite.com), find the American equivalents of each of the following British usages. (*Hint:* When searching for a phrase of two or more words, enter the phrase within quotation marks, such as "fairy cake"). You may have to visit several web sites in order to find a clear answer.

British word or phrase	American equivalent
fairy cake	
nappy	
jumper	
car park	
lorry	
petrol	
lollipop man/lady	
chemist	
crisps	
aubergine	

(continued)

Two Countries Divided by a Common Language - - - - - - -

2. Now for each of the following American usages, use an Internet search engine to find the English equivalent.

American word or phrase	British equivalent
cookie	
zucchini	
windshield	
flashlight	
dumpster	
ground beef	
baby carriage	
potato chip	
vacation	
private school	

3. Why do you think these language differences have arisen? List and describe three reasons below.

   •

   •

   •

4. In order to join the legal profession in the United States, a person must first take a "bar examination" to become a lawyer. Lawyers are also members of "bar associations." Using an Internet search engine, find out what lawyers are called in England. Then explain where the American legal system's use of the word "bar" comes from.

Borrowed Words and False Cognates - - - - - - - - - - - - - - - -

A BORROWED WORD is a word that one language borrows from another. Common examples of words borrowed by English from other languages include "rendezvous" (from French), "kindergarten" (from German), and "tycoon" (from Japanese). As we mentioned in Activity 1 in this unit, the word *alphabet* is borrowed from the first two letters of the Greek alphabet, alpha and beta. Additionally, English words that end in the suffixes *-tion, -cracy,* and *-ology* are derived from Greek. These include words such as *commotion, democracy,* and *biology.* Other languages have frequently borrowed from the Greeks. For example, the Spanish and Portuguese word for democracy is *democracia* and the French word for biology is *biologique.* The word *hippopotamus* comes from two Greek words that mean "river horse." In Chinese, the word for *hippopotamus* is *he-ma,* which means river horse.

Record your answers below. Use another sheet of paper, if necessary.

1. Why do you think so many languages have borrowed words from the Greeks? Explain your answer.

Many place names in the United States, including the names of states, rivers, lakes, and communities, come from Native-American words. These include Kentucky (from the Iroquois people), Wyoming (Algonquin), Oklahoma (Choctaw), Connecticut (Mohican), Omaha (Omaha), and Chicago (a Pottawatomie word for "skunk").

2. Explain why many U.S. geographic names are derived from Native-American words.

Words that are similar in many different languages are called **international words.** These tend to be words that are borrowed by many different languages throughout the world. Linguists believe there are fairly few international words—perhaps fewer than a dozen. Some examples of international words include "mama" and "chocolate." The word origin for mama may not have come from any language at all, but from the mouths of babies who did not yet know a language. (The same can be said for the word papa.) Chocolate comes from two words of the Nahuatl language of Central America meaning "water with bitter bean." In many languages today, including languages in Europe and Asia, the word for chocolate in quite similar in sound to

(continued)

Borrowed Words and False Cognates - - - - - - - - - - - - -

the English word. For example, the Chinese characters for chocolate, 巧克力, sound very similar to the English word when spoken.

3. Why do you think the word chocolate became an international word? Explain your answer.

There are countless words borrowed by one language from other languages. However, one must beware of false cognates, also called "false friends." These are words that sound similar to English words, and may have come from the same borrowed word, but have a different meaning in English. For example, in French, the word *raisin* means "grape." The French term for the English word "raisin" is *raisin sec* (which translates to "dry grape"). A Spanish *libreria* is a bookstore; the Spanish word for library is *biblioteca*. You certainly would not ask for a "pickle" in a restaurant in Germany, where the word *pickel* means a zit!

4. Using an Internet search engine such as Google (google.com) or Excite (excite.com), find out why the following words in English have false cognates in other languages.

   - magazine (What does *magazin* mean in Russian?)

   - gymnasium (What does the word mean in Swedish?)

   - is (What does the word mean in Norwegian?)

   - gift (Why should you refuse a *gift* if someone offers you one in Germany?)

   - entrée (When would one be served an entrée in an American restaurant? When would one be served an *entrée* in a French restaurant?)

Cambodians and Khmer -

មនុស្សទាំងអស់កើតមកមានសេរីភាពនិងភាពស្មើៗគ្នាក្នុងសិទ្ធិនិងសេចក្ដីថ្លៃថ្នូរ ។ មនុស្សគ្រប់
រូបសុទ្ធតែមានវិចារណញ្ញាណនិងសតិសម្បជញ្ញៈ ហើយត្រូវប្រព្រឹត្តចំពោះគ្នាទៅវិញទៅមកក្នុងស្មារតី
រាប់អានគ្នាជាបងប្អូន ។

All human beings are born free and equal in dignity and rights. They are endowed with reason and conscience and should act towards one another in a spirit of brotherhood.
(Article 1 of the Universal Declaration of Human Rights)[1]

CAMBODIA, IN SOUTHEAST ASIA between Vietnam and Thailand, is about the same size as the state of Oklahoma. The nation has a population of about 13.2 million people. Cambodians have their own language, called Khmer (pronounced ka-MER) and their own alphabet, which has thirty-three consonants and twenty-six vowels. It is believed that about eighty percent of Cambodian males age fifteen and over can read and write. Approximately sixty percent of females age fifteen and over can read and write. Some older Cambodians read and write French, as Cambodia was a French colony from 1863 until 1953.

The greatest threat to Cambodian literacy and much more importantly, to Cambodian people's lives, occurred during the 1970s. The dictator Pol Pot and his political group, the Khmer Rouge, took over the country in 1975. Pol Pot sought to turn back the clock on modern civilization and return Cambodia to a land of primitive farming. (Pol Pot spoke of taking the country to "Year Zero.") Phnom Penh, Cambodia's capital and largest city, was emptied by the Khmer Rouge, and its residents led to the rural countryside.

The people who had been educated were subject to torture and often killed. The national library was emptied of its books and turned into a horse stable. By the time Pol Pot was forced from power in 1979, millions of Cambodians had been murdered in the infamous "killing fields."

Record your answers below. Use another sheet of paper, if necessary.

1. The Khmer Rouge sought out people who wore glasses or owned ballpoint pens. These people were often killed. Why do you think the Khmer Rouge targeted these people? Explain your answer.

---

[1] Found at omniglot.com

(continued)

Activity 4 *(continued)*

Cambodians and Khmer ------------------------------

2. Few political leaders in the world have been as brutal as Pol Pot was. However, other political leaders have demonstrated a fear of educated, literate people. Why do you think some political leaders in the world fear people who are literate and educated? Explain your answer.

Today, there is some concern that the Cambodian language may eventually vanish. Young Cambodians, even if literate in Khmer, often listen to music from other countries. Most of the television programs shown in Cambodia are broadcast in the languages of other Asian cultures or in English. Cambodia is a relatively small and poor country. As a result, there is little interest among the world's book and magazine publishers, movie studios, or television companies to produce publications, movies, and programs in Cambodian's native Khmer language.

3. Do you think Cambodians should be afraid of losing their native language? Explain why or why not.

4. What else is lost when a language is lost? Explain your answer.

Literacy and Voting ------------------------------

IN 1994, THE REPUBLIC OF SOUTH AFRICA held its first truly democratic election. Many black South Africans were allowed to vote for the first time. The official ballot for the election was printed in color. The logo for each of the nineteen political parties was displayed, as well as a photograph of each party's leader. The only instruction on the ballot said, "Make your mark next to the party you choose." This instruction appeared in English and eleven other languages. The election was held over several days, giving voters the chance to vote when they did not have to be at work.

Compare this South African election with an American election. Elections in the United States are often held on Tuesdays, a working day for most Americans. The typical American ballot lists the names of each candidate (and political party, if applicable) in black ink on white paper, with no photographs or other distinctive markings. Voters also often vote on referenda, sometimes called "propositions." These propositions, which may change existing laws or add new ones, are often lengthy and written in complex sentences with big words in them.

In 1965, the U.S. Congress passed the Voting Rights Act. This law forbids states from using literacy tests as a means of qualifying voters. Ten years later, Congress passed the Voting Rights Act of 1975. This law required certain state and local governments to provide ballots and other election materials in other languages in addition to English. Those languages include Spanish, several Asian languages, and several Native-American languages.

Record your answers below. Use another sheet of paper, if necessary.

1. Most people believe that some states required voters to pass a literacy test as a way of disqualifying or discouraging poor people from voting.

    • Why do you think they say this?

    • Do you agree that this may have been the intent? Explain why or why not.

    • Why might some of the politicians in a state want to discourage poor people of that state from voting? Explain your answer.

(continued)

Literacy and Voting —

2. A person who was born in another country and is not a United States citizen must take a written test in English in order to become an American citizen. The test includes such questions as, "What are the forty-ninth and fiftieth states of the union?" and "Can you name the two U.S. senators from your state?" A person who is born in the United States and is an American citizen at birth does not have to take this test.

   • Do you think that you would do well on the citizenship exam? Explain why or why not.

   • Do you think that it is important for a United States citizen to know which states were the forty-ninth and fiftieth admitted to the United States? Explain why or why not.

   • Do you think that it is important for a United States citizen to be able to name the two United States senators from one's state? Explain why or why not.

In order to vote legally in the United States, a person must be a United States citizen, either by birth or by having passed a citizenship exam. However, the Voting Rights Act of 1975 requires some state and local governments to print ballots in other languages in addition to English. For example, California prints ballots in English, Chinese, Japanese, Korean, Spanish, Tagalog (the language used by many Filipino Americans), and Vietnamese.

3. Why do you think that some United States citizens are more comfortable voting with ballots in a language other than English? Explain your answer.

(continued)

Literacy and Voting -

4. In November 2002, California voters went to the polls. One of the issues they had to consider was Proposition 47, the Kindergarten–University Public Education Facilities Bond Act of 2002. Here is a small part of the wording of that proposition:

> Notwithstanding any other provision of this chapter, or of the State General Obligation Bond Law, if the Treasurer sells bonds pursuant to this chapter that include a bond counsel opinion to the effect that the interest on the bonds is excluded from gross income for federal tax purposes, subject to designated conditions, the Treasurer may maintain separate accounts for the investment of bond proceeds and for the investment earnings on those proceeds. The Treasurer may use or direct the use of those proceeds or earnings to pay any rebate, penalty, or other payment required under federal law or take any other action with respect to the investment and use of those bond proceeds required or desirable under federal law to maintain the tax-exempt status of those bonds and to obtain any other advantage under federal law on behalf of the funds of this state.

*   Of the 7.7 million Californians who voted in the November 2002 election, 591,062 (over half a million) did not bother to vote either for or against Proposition 47. Why do you think so many voters decided not to vote one way or another on this proposition? Explain your answer.

*   Do you think that the average voter understood what this part of Proposition 47 meant?

(continued)

Literacy and Voting — — — — — — — — — — — — — — — — — —

Shown below is a ballot used in an election in Connecticut in 2003.

STATE OF CONNECTICUT OFFICIAL ABSENTEE BALLOT	West Hartford, Connecticut	District	Municipal Election	Date of Election November 4, 2003

Be sure to read instructions on reverse side before marking this ballot.

Write in Votes ➡	1	2	3	4	5	6	7	8	9
Vote on the Question ➡									

OFFICE ➡ / PARTY ⬇	1	2	3	4	5	6	7	8	9
		Town Council Vote for any six					Town Clerk	Board of Education Vote for any two	
REPUBLICAN	Joe Verrngia ☐ 1A	Carl Donatelli ☐ 2A	Kevin Connors ☐ 3A	Barbara Carpenter ☐ 4A	Rob Bouvier ☐ 5A	Al Turco ☐ 6A	7A	Naogan Ma ☐ 8A	Tom Fiorentino ☐ 9A
DEMOCRATIC	Maureen Kelly McClay ☐ 1B	Art Spada ☐ 2B	Scott Slitka ☐ 3B	Carolyn Thornberry ☐ 4B	Chuck Coursey ☐ 5B	Jonathan Harris ☐ 6B	Norma W. Cronin ☐ 7B	Bruce Putterman ☐ 8B	Terry Schmitt ☐ 9B
	1C	2C	3C	4C	5C	6C	7C	8C	9C
	1D	2D	3D	4D	5D	6D	7D	8D	9D

5. Which election method do you prefer?

- The South African method, with voters given several days to get to the polls and a ballot with color photographs of the candidates as discussed on page 106, or

- The one day election with the plain written ballot commonly used in the United States, such as the ballot shown above. Explain your answer.

Which Font Do You Want? ---------------------------

A TYPEFACE is the design of lettering. One basic distinction in typefaces is between **serif** and **sans serif** type. Serif type has little lines on the edges of most letters:

Serif

Sans serif type does not have these little lines ("sans" is the French word for "without"):

Sans serif

When a typeface is slanted (usually, to the right) it is called *italicized.* Italics help provide emphasis in text. They can also help create the sense of movement.

When a typeface is made heavier and thicker than normal, it is called **boldface.**

The size of a typeface is measured in points. This is 12 point type. This is 6 point type.

This is 18 point type.

The particular size and style of a typeface is called a *font.* The font of the text printed in this book is 12 point Futura T.

One concern that **typographers,** graphic designers, and printers have is the readability of a font. Some typefaces are easier to read in larger sizes. These are often called display typefaces. **This is an example of a display typeface.** A display typeface may be good for a large sign, but not as effective if used for the text in a book or magazine. Display typefaces are often sans serif. Serif typefaces are often used for text material. This is because serifs help connect the letters together in the reader's mind as she or he reads the text. Another thing to consider is the mood that a typeface creates for the reader. This is where you come in. You have been asked to choose the best typeface for each of the following applications. Next to each application, write which typeface you chose from the list on page 111. Explain why you chose that typeface for each application. (You can use each typeface only once.)

Record your answers below. Use another sheet of paper, if necessary.

1. The nameplate that will appear on a new Cadillac car model that is aimed primarily at people between the ages of fifty and sixty-five

2. The nameplate that will appear on a new Honda car model that is aimed primarily at people between the ages of eighteen and thirty

(continued)

Which Font Do You Want? -

3. The sign on the front of a funeral home

4. The sign on the front of a restaurant that serves Mexican food

5. The nameplate that will appear on the front of a new video game machine

6. The name that will appear on the label of a new brand of a lemon-lime flavored soft drink

7. A greeting card used by parents to announce the birth of their new baby

8. The title font on the cover of a new hip-hop magazine

𝔉ont 1	Font 7
Font 2	Font 8
Font 3	Font 9
FONT 4	Font 10
Font 5	FONT 11
Font 6	Font 12

boldface—a typeface heavier and thicker than normal

design element—a mark or an arrangement of marks in a document or on an object. Color can also be a design element. A design element often conveys meaning, even though it may not rely on words to do so.

diacritical mark—a small symbol above or below letters that tells the reader how a letter is to be pronounced or how syllables in a word are stressed. Also called a *diacritic*.

icon—a person, an image, or a symbol that represents part of a larger theme in society. The Statue of Liberty is an example of an icon.

international word—a word that is similar in sound and meaning in many different languages. "Chocolate" is among the dozen words believed to be international words.

linguist—a person who studies languages. Linguists analyze the similarities and differences between languages, and the reasons for those similarities and differences.

logo—a symbol used as the identifying mark of a company. Among the more famous logos are McDonald's golden arches.

sans serif—a type of lettering that does not contain serifs.

serif—the small lines that appear on some types of lettering. Serifs generally provide a more formal appearance to a letter. Serifs also help readers move their eyes, as the small lines move our eyes in a horizontal line.

theme—an idea or a concept. A theme is often visually represented by an icon. "Freedom" is an example of an important theme in American culture.

typographer—a person who designs lettering, or selects types of lettering for different applications.

Additional Resources

Books

Arnheim, Rudolf, *Visual Thinking* (London: Faber, 1970).

Berger, John, *Ways of Seeing* (New York: Penguin, 1972).

Gardner, Howard, *The Arts and Human Development: A Psychological Study of the Artistic Process* (New York: Wiley, 1973).

Kaiser, Ward L., *Seeing Through Maps: The Power of Images to Shape Our World View* (Amherst, Mass: ODT Inc., 2001).

Kitch, Carolyn L., *The Girl on the Magazine Cover: The Origins of Visual Stereotypes in American Mass Media* (Chapel Hill: University of North Carolina Press, 2001).

McCarthy, Anna, *Ambient Television: Visual Culture and Public Space* (Durham, N.C.: Duke University Press, 2001).

Mirzoeff, Nicholas, *An Introduction to Visual Culture* (London: Routledge, 1999).

Tufte, Edward R., *The Visual Display of Quantitative Information,* second edition (Cheshire, Connecticut: Graphics Press, 2001).

Web Sites

Alphabets of the World
word2word.com/alphabet.html

Cinema Therapy
cinematherapy.com

The Color Marketing Group, a not-for-profit association of color professionals:
colormarketing.org

Evolution of Alphabets
wam.umd.edu/~rfradkin/alphapage.html

A Guide to Writing Systems
omniglot.com

Luscher Color Test, a psychological perspective on colors and personality
supervert.com/shockwave/colortest/

Share Your Bright Ideas

We want to hear from you!

Your name_____Date_____

School name_____

School address_____

City _____State _____Zip_____Phone number (_____)_____

Grade level(s) taught_____Subject area(s) taught_____

Where did you purchase this publication?_____

In what month do you purchase a majority of your supplements?_____

What moneys were used to purchase this product?

_____School supplemental budget   _____Federal/state funding   _____Personal

Please "grade" this Walch publication in the following areas:

Quality of service you received when purchasing	A	B	C	D
Ease of use	A	B	C	D
Quality of content	A	B	C	D
Page layout	A	B	C	D
Organization of material	A	B	C	D
Suitability for grade level	A	B	C	D
Instructional value	A	B	C	D

COMMENTS:_____

_____

What specific supplemental materials would help you meet your current—or future—instructional needs?

_____

Have you used other Walch publications? If so, which ones?_____

May we use your comments in upcoming communications?   _____Yes   _____No

Please **FAX** this completed form to **888-991-5755**, or mail it to

Customer Service, Walch Publishing, P. O. Box 658, Portland, ME 04104-0658

We will send you a **FREE GIFT** in appreciation of your feedback. **THANK YOU!**